ENCOUNTERS WITH ANGELS

Encounters with

ANGELS

L.W. NORTHRUP

Tyndale House
Publishers, Inc.
Wheaton, Illinois

Scripture quotations are from the King James
Version of the Bible.

First printing, June 1988

Library of Congress Catalog Card
Number 88-50179
ISBN 0-8423-0765-6
Copyright 1988 by L. W. Northrup
All rights reserved
Printed in the United States of America

To my dear wife, Clara,
who has borne with so much love and patience
my frequent absences,
and to all my loving family,
who have known that I need a guardian angel.
And to my dear sister,
Merrie Claire Adler, R.N.,
who has accompanied me on many trips to Bible lands
and has ministered to me and many others
with her wonderful nursing skills
and has often been, indeed,
an "angel unawares."

CONTENTS

PREFACE

The book you are holding is about the work of angels around the globe — work that I have personally witnessed. God's angels are everywhere upon the earth, and I have been privileged as a world traveler to see their ministry in my own life at various places around this vast world. Perhaps I should begin with a word about how I came to be such a traveler.

As a child I had a wealthy uncle who went each winter to the great Pacific Northwest. He returned like one of Israel's spies from that promised land, bearing pictures of himself sitting on gigantic tree stumps and eating enormous apples and peaches. My youthful fancy was completely captured — I determined to reach that paradise at any cost. At the age of sixteen, in 1923, I boarded a train in Brainerd, Minnesota, and bade farewell forever to forty-below-zero weather and mountainous drifts of snow. I enrolled at what was then called Seattle Pacific College as its youngest student. When I arrived in Seattle I knew I was on the borderline of heaven itself. But I was destined to travel much further than Seattle.

In 1954, I went with a group from Asbury College for five weeks to the Bible lands and Europe. This trip changed my whole life. From that point I was a hopeless travel addict. My travels have led me into over sixty countries of the world, to all the states of the U.S., to nearly all of the provinces of Canada, and to most of the mission fields of my church, the Free Methodists. As a tour leader and traveler I have been to Israel twenty times and led scores of pilgrims to the Bible lands, to Africa, and to Europe.

My little grandson Timmy has said that his grandpa is a "born traveler." Many people have asked this "born traveler" to write a book about his travels. Perhaps now the time has come to select some of the most striking incidents and observations that may interest readers, especially travelers.

My primary aim in telling these stories is not to delight the reader with travel tales, but to glorify the Lord. I have found His promise so true through the millions of miles that I have traveled: "Behold, I send an angel before thee to keep thee in the way, and to bring thee into the place which I have prepared" (Exod. 23:20). Doubtless, the Lord saw how much I needed that angelic protection. I confess that I have a poor sense of direction. When I see a sign that says "Right," I often find myself going left. If I come to a door that says "Push," I may find myself pulling it. Sometimes I have gone many miles out of my way while driving by making a wrong turn at a crucial highway intersection. It is a peculiar and distressing tendency. Also, I am not attentive to details. While I admire perfectionists, I am not one of them. Too often I find that I have omitted some very vital point in carrying out my plans. Regrettably, I lack the ability to make quick decisions, which can be disastrous, especially in traveling. A demand for a prompt answer to a sudden question can easily throw me into confusion. I find myself responding slowly, often to the irritation of the questioner.

With these problems one might wonder how I ever survived a lifetime of frequent exposure to difficult experiences. My daughters have always said, "Dad, you have a guardian angel." I do not wonder, because I know there has been an angel guiding me in the midst of life-threatening decisions. I do not look upon these experiences as simply "blundering through," but I can say with Peter, "There stood by me this night the angel of God, whose I am, and whom I serve" (Acts 27:23).

This book is a recital of the acts of a God who really cares, and who has at His disposal an infinite number of heavenly messengers to carry out His loving designs for His children. Before I begin my own story of how I have seen the Lord's angels at work, I wish to address a critical question: Are there really angels today, and what are they like? I choose to draw my answers to this from the most obvious source, the Holy Scriptures.

"The angel of the Lord encampeth round about them that fear him, and delivereth them" (Psa. 34:7).

PART ONE
Angels, Indeed, in the Modern World

ONE
BELIEVING IN ANGELS
IN A SKEPTICAL AGE

Albert Einstein was sometimes described as an intensely religious person. He spoke and wrote of having a "cosmic religion." He spoke scornfully of "professional atheists." He was said to have "a rapturous amazement at the harmony of natural law, which reveals an intelligence of such superiority that compared with it, all the systematic thinking and acting of human beings is an utterly insignificant reflection."

He might be suspected of almost being a believer in God at times. He wrote, "A person who is religiously enlightened appears to me to be the one who has, to the best of his ability, liberated himself from the fetters of his selfish desires, and is preoccupied with thoughts, feelings, and aspirations to which he clings because of their super-personal value." Here, indeed are some thoughts which might be stated by the Christian faith.

Einstein's God, however, was the universe. Our admiration of Einstein's religiosity is dimmed when we read what he said in 1931: "I cannot conceive of a God who rewards and punishes its creatures or has a will of the kind we experience in ourselves. Neither can I, nor would I want to conceive of an individual that survives his physical death."

Einstein was a pantheist. He did not believe that God was anything more than the mysterious harmony of the universe. This is the impersonal God that he worshiped with such beautiful senti-ments. This notion of God may allure the scientist and the agnos-tic, but it offers no consolation to God's creatures who so desperately need His help. Ultimately, pantheism is no more satisfying to human beings than outright atheism. For life to have meaning and hope, human beings need a personal God.

We believe in a personal God, a God who really cares for his crea-tures. With this God in mind, we begin to look at the reality of angels.

IS THIS A LIVE ISSUE?

Is the subject of angels, or *angelology,* too hot to handle? Do we rush in "where angels fear to tread?" Or is the subject too *cold* to handle — a dead issue that no serious modern person has any interest in? Why is so little spoken, written, or debated about such an appealing subject?

A few centuries ago the subject of angels was a rich part of the culture of our world. The importance of angels would never have been questioned. Three great faiths — Islam, Judaism, and Chris-tianity — held it as a dogma of their systems of religious thought. Zoroastrianism came not far behind.

But angelology is no longer a subject of major inquiry among theologians. The answers to why this is so are not too difficult to discover.

First, when Soviet cosmonauts first returned from orbiting the earth, they announced triumphantly that they hadn't found any God out there. This corroborated their atheistic philosophy. They were probably looking for a being with a long, white beard, sitting upon a throne of some kind, surrounded by a cloud of Byzantine glory, worshiped by winged beings. This concept of heaven somewhere in outer space has been disproven by scientific exploration, but to our minds nothing concrete has been presented to substitute for that age-old, comforting image of heaven and angels. We just aban-doned the angels or quit thinking about them altogether.

Second, humanistic philosophy has been so universally believed that many people can conceive of only one world instead of two.

16

They live completely in the domain of the visible. Death, we think, ends it all. God does not exist, or, if he does, he plays no real role in the world.

Third, another reason why angelology has been a dead issue is the substitution of extraterrestrial creatures for the angels. In spite of all our dazzling advances in science and technology, man cannot seem to shake the belief in beings of a superhuman order. It seems that many people — and many of these are educated, intelligent types — believe that other planets are inhabited and that almost any day now we are to expect an invasion from outer space of friendly or unfriendly creatures. Films like *E.T.* and *Close Encounters of the Third Kind* have been extremely popular. People seem to want to believe that UFOs hum around in the atmosphere above us, carrying who knows what cargoes of extraterrestrial invaders. While many people still believe these interplanetary visitors may be extremely hostile, the current emphasis is on amiable creatures. Apparently people like to think that there are benevolent, intelligent creatures out beyond earth, waiting to be good to us. The very popular 1984 film *2010* played on this idea; at the film's center was an unidentified "force" — not a personal God, of course — that saved the world from nuclear war.

In October 1985 it was reported that six Soviet cosmonauts said they had witnessed the most inspiring spectacle ever encountered in space: a band of glowing angels — seven giant figures in the form of humans, but with wings and mistlike halos, and in the classic depiction of angels. They appeared to be hundreds of feet tall with wingspans as great as a jetliner. The apparitions followed the cosmonauts around for about ten minutes and then vanished as quickly as they had come. A report in the April 6, 1986 issue of a national tabloid paper spoke of the incident: "Reports that Soviet cosmonauts sighted a band of angels on a space mission last summer have been disputed by a Russian researcher who says the celestial apparitions were actually fields of pure energy and alien intellect." In an interview with French journalist Andre Demazure, Dr. Yuri Manakov said the cosmonauts initially referred to the beings as angels simply because the beings had wings. "But now that all the facts are in, he said, there can be no doubt: The creatures descended from a race of humanoids who shed their bodies after reaching the top of the evolutionary ladder. I have studied every aspect of the cosmonauts' report and this is my conclusion," said the astrophysicist. "I realize that Christians around the world would like to believe that this phenomenon is proof of their God in heaven. But as Communists, as atheists, we Soviets take a purely scientific approach. We have not let religious superstition distort the facts. And we say these beings are far from angels even if they did have wings." So even though atheists on both sides of the ocean may not believe in angels, they choose to believe in some preposterous extraterrestrial beings.

Fourth, angels have been degraded by childish notions and comic misrepresentation. An eminent modern preacher and theologian said caustically in one of his characteristic statements, "We need to get Christ out of the cow-barn." Perhaps we should get those cute little angels off the Christmas tree as well!

Karl Barth, the great modern theologian, stated that he detested paintings that depict "the infant Jesus with a veritable kindergarten of prancing babies amusing themselves in different ways and yet all contriving in some way to look pious. Even more offensive are Raphael's little darlings." Adam Clarke, the great Bible commentator, says that the cute infant angels are "the worst of commentators." It debases the angels to caricature them as comic creatures, playthings of fancy, or infantile creatures. In the chain of being, they are higher than man and stand in the presence of God.

Intelligent people are probably right to reject the image of angels as cute, pudgy babies. Certainly there is nothing in Scripture to support such an image. The Bible indicates that angels often appear as imposing, magnificent creatures, not grinning infants.

Fifth, to others, the very loss of angels is irrelevant. "So what if there are angels? What does that mean to me?" Religious thinking, especially of a serious nature, is completely out of their sphere of existence. They have never given it any thought, and they do not plan to do so. Eternal things have no place in the philosophy of life of such individuals, much less winged beings (as they caricature them) flying around in the air.

Sixth, when one wishes to turn the subject of angelology off quickly he says, "How many angels can dance on the head of a pin?"

This reference to a supposed discussion in the Middle Ages is designed to close the discussion. We have heard this hypothetical question scornfully used countless times. This question was credited to Thomas Aquinas of Middle Ages fame. Actually this question, which is supposed to dismiss all rational inquiry, was never asked by him or by anyone else. It is only a cop-out for moderns who wish to avoid any serious contemplation of angelology.

The medieval theologians were, actually, very interested in angels. Even today there is a *Dictionary of Angels* in which are listed in great numbers the wonderful creatures of medieval theology. Moderns compliment themselves as having escaped this type of thought forever. The literature of the Middle Ages was filled with the wildest speculations and fantasies of all sorts. Yet where would the museums of this world be without the marvelous ingenuity and beauty that those very studies produced? They would be barren, indeed.

Finally, the study of angelology is too cold to handle perhaps because we live in such an affluent society. In the time when the saints faced the mouths of lions and the fires of martyrdom, they believed in angels. They needed them. If tomorrow the KGB or some other heinous weapon of the state were to knock at our door, we might be more interested in angels.

FILLING A SPIRITUAL VACUUM

In spite of the neglect of angelology, mankind cannot seem to live without belief in the existence of a spirit or spiritual world, a world where both good and evil beings have an effect on man and his history. There is a multitude of religious beliefs in the world, but all religions, even that modern religion that we can only know by the name of *secularism,* exhibit some belief in the spiritual realm. The beings of this spiritual world have been variously referred to as aeons, demons, demigods, genii, angels, and many other names.

The belief in these superhuman creatures has been universal, and many religious systems have had very highly developed beliefs in angels. The Persian Zoroastrians did, and some scholars believe that under Persian influence the Jews developed their views on angels. There is no conclusive evidence for this, however.

Whether highly developed or rudimentary, the belief in super-human beings is present throughout the world. Even in a world where people mock organized religion and traditional expressions of spirituality, the belief that the unseen and supernatural can be experienced persists. The mysterious powers of ESP (extrasensory perception) baffle scientific analysis. Its powers have been subjected to merciless scrutiny. Universities have established centers to study it. Telepathy, prophecy, and psychokinesis are tempting fields of study. These possibilities of the mind are challenging hitherto accepted scientific finalities. Even the Russians are now investigating ESP. On a recent trip to Israel I encountered a group of about thirty people who were studying pyramidology. They were on their way to Egypt to explore the mystical message of the Great Pyramid. They were confident that in the bowels of that massive mountain of stone was the blueprint for the future. These tendencies prevail everywhere on the world scene, yet the materialistic thought of our day has largely rejected the biblical message of angelology.

Man cannot live in a spiritual vacuum. Once true religion, including belief in God's angels, has been discarded, the occult rushes in. The occult's many forms — astrology, ESP, witchcraft, black magic, fortune telling, Satan worship — have become worldwide phenomena.

It would appear from this trend that society has developed a tremendous appetite for the supernatural. Interest in these areas has risen and spread like an epidemic. In France and Germany there are thousands of sorcerers taking in millions of dollars (and people) every year. Tens of thousands believe in witches. In my travels in Europe, attempting to present Christ, I found rejection. I was simply told that they did not believe; in Denmark for instance, the young people apparently did not even know what a church was.

Many see in this acceptance of the occult a judgment of God. Paul says in Romans 1:21, "Because that, when they knew God, they glorified him not as God, neither were thankful; but became vain in their imaginations, and their foolish heart was darkened."

A great archaeologist and theologian, Dr. Merrill Unger, writes, "This human spirit does possess mysterious powers, but the greater power of demonic spirits to delude humanity is the unrecognized peril surrounding parapsychologists and spiritualists."

Dr. Billy Graham, in his book *Angels: God's Secret Agents,* says that a Gallup poll has revealed that 70 percent of Americans believe there is a devil, and he is a scary person. The popular book *People of the Lie* by Christian psychiatrist M. Scott Peck contained a chilling account of two exorcisms the author had observed. Dr. Peck, writing both to Christians and to religionless moderns, confirmed that demons do indeed inhabit human bodies in the modern world.

One might think that such accounts, written by serious, rational men, might have the effect of turning faithless people to God. But Satan, being cunning, employs a two-pronged attack on people. The first is to convince the intellectually minded materialist that he does not exist. This he has done very successfully for a long time. Under this guise of nonexistence he can do his subtle work very powerfully. The other stratagem is used to convince those without true religion that he is a being of tremendous power, too fearful to oppose. This controls the heathen mind by creating enormous fear and a willingness to submit to any and all of Satan's artifices. In either way, Satan's work is done.

AN ALTERNATIVE TO DEMONS

This is a book about angels, and particularly about guardian angels, not about demons. I chose to mention belief in demons because it attests to the spiritual void that many people feel today. I will aim to show that the unseen, the supernatural, is not, contrary to contemporary belief, solely the realm of Satan and his minions.

Even in our secular age it is common to use the term *angel,* though it is used very, very loosely, with no more serious faith than we would have when we speak of Santa Claus or leprechauns. We can never experience the true blessing of the ministry of angels until we obtain a clearer image of these majestic creatures.

The Bible speaks often about angels, particularly in relation to the life of Christ. Their ministry is inextricably interwoven with the divine activity both in the Old Testament and the New Testament.

The Sadducees said there was no resurrection, no angels, no spirit. They challenged Jesus, and he replied that their ignorance of the subject lay in the fact that they did "err, not knowing the Scriptures, nor the power of God" (Matt. 22:29).

Many people, even Christians, know little about angels. In the next chapter we will look at what has been taught through the ages about angels, and at what the Bible says about them. I hope this will remedy some of our ignorance about angels and about the power of God so that we will not be guilty of being twentieth-century Sadducees.

TWO
WHAT ANGELS ARE REALLY LIKE

What are angels really like, and how do they communicate with mankind as they are reported to have done in Scripture, and by countless individual testimonials?

Christianity itself has often been guilty of too much extrabiblical speculation about the nature of angels. Through the ages hundreds of artists have portrayed angels as beings with physical bodies, bodies that are not always based on the biblical accounts. The influence of medieval theology, which inspired the great poetry of Dante and Milton, the famous paintings of Titian and Raphael, as well as scores of the world's greatest artists, has left mankind a legacy of marvelous beauty, though it has often had no real basis in the Bible. The beautiful icons of the Byzantine world show angels as intense, masculine beings in courtly or military dress. These images are not too far from the biblical picture, since the Bible indicates that the angels function as court servants and soldiers of the heavenly king, God. But the effeminate — sometimes juvenile — angels in many paintings from the Renaissance on are certainly far from the awe-inspiring angels of the Bible. The child angels are cute and endearing, but they do little to inspire awe and piety. It is these appealing — but unbiblical — images that linger in many people's minds. (Luckily there have been some signs of change; the famous sculpture of the archangel Michael on the reconstructed cathedral in Coventry, England, shows a powerful, masculine angel treading down Satan.)

One reason that artists began to portray angels as infants or as soft, effeminate figures is that such portrayals made angels more approachable, less fearsome. And perhaps another reason is that there emerged some writings which departed from the biblical witness. In the Middle Ages a dramatic attempt was made to describe the angels. The earliest attempt at this was a magnificent performance by a man who wrote under the pseudonym of Dionysius the Areopagite, the Dionysius of Athens mentioned in the Book of Acts (17:34). Though we now believe that this author was a monk living in Syria, probably in the sixth century, he wrote under the name of Paul's first convert in Athens. Until his writings appeared, no Christian had ever attempted to produce a systematic structure of the angelic hosts. He gave the world the book *The Celestial Hierarchy*. He drew on Paul's statements in Ephesians and Colossians to construct a nine-tiered organization of the angels. These nine orders were, in descending order, seraphim, cherubim, thrones, dominions, virtues, powers, principalities, archangels, and angels. In Dionysius's system the orders did not differ in moral perfection — only in their function in the divine economy of grace and glory of God. However, all of these existed under one generic name of *angels.*

In the Scriptures no organization of this kind appears. But the greatest leaders of the church accepted Dionysius's work as truth. His concept of the nine-storied heavenly angelic state was a spiritual, architectural masterpiece of angelology. It captured Thomas Aquinas, the superb theologian-philosopher of the Middle Ages. He completely accepted it, and devoted a whole chapter to it in his famous *Summa Theologica*. Since Thomas's theology was extremely influential in the church for centuries, the thought of Dionysius filtered down to the clergy and influenced their beliefs about angels. While the artists were gradually prettifying the angels, Dionysius's influence was making the angels seem less and less interested in man's affairs. Thanks to the artists and to Dionysius, the angels in people's imaginations were quite different from the angels in Scripture.

As the leaders of the Reformation saw, Dionysius had dealt with angels apart from the biblical witness. The Reformers also came to believe — correctly — that this Dionysius was not really the person mentioned as Paul's convert.

WHAT DOES THE BIBLE SAY ABOUT ANGELS?

The Reformers, trying to ground all belief in the Bible, knew that beliefs about angels had to be based on Scripture, not on the elaborate speculations of Dionysius. Fortunately, they found that the Bible does have much to say about angels.

The Bible speaks about angels 273 times — 108 times in the Old Testament, 165 times in the New Testament. To reject angels is to reject the Bible. A disbelief in angels implies a disbelief in Christ Himself.

One of the keys to a proper understanding of angels is that we understand their specific function. The Hebrew word *malach* means "messenger," and so does the Greek word in the New Testament, *angelos*. Both words can be applied to human messengers, but the contexts of the passages clearly indicates whether a man or an angelic being is being referred to.

Angels in the Bible are a superhuman order of heavenly beings, and the 273 references in the Bible indicate this. The Bible indicates that these superhuman beings are created by God — they are not gods in their own right. Psalm 148:2, 5, makes it clear that they are *creatures*: "Praise ye him, all his angels; praise ye him, all his host. . . . Let them praise the name of the Lord; for he commanded, and they were created." Paul also mentions their creaturely status: "For by him were all things created, that are in heaven, and that are in earth, visible and invisible, whether they be thrones, or dominions, or principalities, or powers: all things were created by him, and for him" (Col. 1:16).

The names *thrones, dominions, principalities,* and *powers* refer to angelic beings. The Scripture writers also use other names when referring to angels. Abraham perceived them as "three men" (Gen. 18:2), while Jacob greeted angels as "God's host" (Gen. 32:2). The psalmist refers to them as the "holy ones" (Ps. 89:7). In Job they are referred to as the "sons of God" (Job 1:6; 38:7). Daniel, referring to their office of serving God, presents them as "watchers" (Dan. 4:13) and as "princes" (Dan. 10:13). The Epistle to the Hebrews also refers to them as "ministering spirits" (Heb. 1:14). But most often they are referred to as angels.

Since angels are creatures, students of the Bible have speculated about when they were created. The Book of Job seems to indicate that they were created before the world: "Where wast thou when I [God] laid the foundations of the earth? . . . When the morning stars sang together, and all the sons of God shouted for joy?" (Job 38:4, 7). The Bible does not make it clear just how long the angels existed before the world began, but then, that is not important. What is important is that, in spite of their being creatures of a higher order than man, they are still vastly inferior to God. Though they are superhuman, they are not, strictly speaking, divine in their own right.

Amazing powers are attributed to angels. The woman of Tekoa, praising King David's wisdom, acknowledges "my lord is wise, according to the wisdom of an angel of God, to know all things that are in the earth" (2 Sam. 14:20). Jesus also implied that their knowledge was great, though limited: "But of that day and hour [the time of his return] knoweth no man, no, not the angels of heaven, but my Father only" (Matt. 24:36). They are not only intelligent but strong: "Behold, there was a great earthquake; for the angel of the Lord descended from heaven, and came and rolled back the stone from the door, and sat upon it" (Matt. 28:2).

Angels are always associated with the idea of goodness and holiness, and the Bible implies that they were indeed created holy and good. In Genesis 1:31, God surveys all his creation and pronounces it good; this would indicate that everything, including the angels, was good. But many passages indicate that some angels fell into sin, the chief of whom was Satan (see Jude 6; Isa. 14:12-15; Ezek. 28:11-19). No one knows how this could happen. One wonders how holy, superhuman beings could turn to evil. But the Bible does imply that the angels who did not follow Satan remained holy and obedient to God. In 1 Timothy 5:21, Paul refers to "elect angels," making it clear that they are distinct from the fallen angels.

Much speculation has occurred about the *ranks* of angels. The

words used by Paul — *thrones, dominions, powers,* and *principalities* —
are usually taken to refer to different orders of angels. Dionysius's
The Celestial Hierarchy influenced many later generations of Christian thinkers, but the Bible gives no evidence about such a hierarchy. However, it is clear that the rank of *archangel* does exist, and
that rank is held by Michael (Jude 9). Michael appears in Revelation 12:7, where he is waging war in heaven against the dragon. The
angel Gabriel is mentioned by name in the Bible, and he has a special role in conveying God's messages to Daniel, to Zacharias, and
to Mary. Because of his exalted role, many people believe that Gabriel
is also an archangel.

Cherubim and *seraphim* are mentioned in the Bible, and we can
assume that these were angelic beings. Isaiah saw seraphim in his
famous vision in the temple (Isa. 6), and the cherubim are mentioned as guarding the tree of life in Eden (Gen. 3:24) and as bearing the chariot-throne of God (Ezek. 10). Images of two cherubim
adorned the ark of the covenant (Exod. 25:18-22) and Solomon's
temple (1 Kings 6:23). Both seraphim and cherubim are presented
as having wings, and they seem to exist in close proximity to God.
These characteristics, and the fact that they are mentioned so often
in Scripture, may mean that they are of a different order than the
rest of the angels. However, their elevated position does not indicate that they were necessarily at the top of any heavenly hierarchy
of angels.

WHAT DO ANGELS DO?

Angels are not beings aimlessly flying around in dense clouds in
the sky or soaring at random in the blue. They are not cute little
cherubs swinging on a Christmas tree, or winged beings depicted
on a greeting card. As the highest of God's created beings, they have
an intimate and unique relationship to God. They present themselves in His presence from time to time and receive instructions
from Him and do His commands (Job 1:6). They express delight
and joy at God's wonderful creation (Job 38:7). One of their chief
occupations is to exalt and praise God's holy name (Ps. 29:1-2).

Angels played many roles in the life of Christ. Angels heralded His birth (Luke 2:10-15), guided and warned His parents (Matt. 2:13), strengthened Him after His temptation (Matt. 4:11) and during His agony in the garden (Luke 22:43), and announced and aided in His resurrection (Matt. 28:2-6). They will announce and accompany Him at the Second Coming (Acts 1:10-11; Matt. 25:31; 1 Thess. 4:16; 2 Thess. 1:7; Rev. 19:14, 17), and they will praise and worship Him as He prepares to inaugurate judgment upon the world (Rev. 5:11-12).

The messages of the angels are not self-conceived, but transmitted by a Sovereign God. The writer of Hebrews says, "the word of angels was steadfast, and every transgression and disobedience receive a just recompense of reward" (Heb. 2:2). Those who ignore the "messengers" court disaster of the highest magnitude.

Most important for this book, however, *angels are a vital link between God and man.* They have awesome responsibilities. The law God gave to man was given through angels (Gal. 3:19). Angels are used by God to make his prophetic program known to man (Dan. 8:16; Rev. 1:1-2). In one dramatic instance of God revealing his message, an angel causes Balaam to bless Israel instead of cursing it (Num. 22:31).

Though used in various activities, they are most occupied with carrying out God's orders on the earth. They are his ministers (Ps. 104:4). They also, as intelligent and holy creatures, display a vital interest in God's plan of salvation; they rejoice over the repentance of even one sinner (Luke 15:10), and they are fascinated at watching the drama of salvation (1 Pet. 1:12).

As a link between God and man, angels especially serve as a link between God and believers. Both the Old and New Testaments show that angels watch over believers and protect their interests. Belief in guardian angels is not an explicit teaching of the Scriptures, but it is obvious from the Bible that the belief is valid, for it is clear that angels do watch over the faithful. Witness such passages as Psalm 34:7 ("The angel of the Lord encampeth round about them that fear him, and delivereth them") and Psalm 91:11 ("For he shall give his angels charge over thee, to keep thee in all thy ways"). Other passages confirm the protective nature of angels. Abraham, in sending his servant to find a wife for Isaac, announced that God would send "his angel before thee, and thou shalt take a wife unto my son from thence." Abraham had learned of angelic protection and guidance when he was stayed from sacrificing Isaac. Lot and Jacob had also learned of angelic protection (Gen. 19:1-15; 28:12).

Later in the Old Testament, God sent an angel to lead His people (Exod. 14:19; 23:20), to provide for the needs of the prophet Elijah (1 Kings 19:5), to deliver His children from the fiery furnace (Dan. 3:28), and to stop the mouths of the lions (Dan. 7:22).

In the New Testament we see that guardianship of angels is made even more clear. Jesus implied that each of us has a guardian angel when He spoke about the young children: "Take heed that ye despise not one of these little ones; for I say unto you, that in heaven their angels do always behold the face of my Father which is in heaven" (Matt. 18:10). The Epistle to the Hebrews, possibly drawing on Christ's teaching asks, "Are they not all ministering spirits, sent forth to minister for them who shall be heirs of salvation?" (Heb. 1:14).

Guardianship is further demonstrated when the apostles are freed from prison by an angel (Acts 5:19), when Peter is delivered by an angel (Acts 12:5-7), and when Paul is encouraged in a time of fear (Acts 27:23-24).

Time and time again God's servants have experienced the protection and guidance of the angels. Do guardian angels still protect believers? Some people say no, for they believe the Holy Spirit takes the place of any present angelic ministry. But others believe that angelic guardianship is very real today. Certainly the Holy Spirit was working in Paul's and Peter's day, yet both apostles experienced the work of angels in their lives. It is my belief—and my own experience as well as the experience of many other contemporary believers affirms this—that angels still guide and protect believers.

Angels do not preach, they only announce. Angels are often portrayed as "singing," and we love to think of "angel choirs." The seraphim in Isaiah's vision are calling out to each other, proclaiming God's holiness (Isa. 6:3), and some Bible readers regard this as singing. In the New Testament, John's vision of heaven includes a scene where all living creatures, angels included, are singing songs of praise to the Lamb (Rev. 5:11-14). When the Bible speaks so often of believers singing their praise to the Lord, it must certainly be true that the angels must sing and make celestial music for God and Christ.

The angels have only to do with the physical needs of mankind. Spiritual matters are not their concern or their responsibility. They do not do the work of the Holy Spirit. They never substitute for the Godhead. They are represented as being observers, not participants, in the plan of salvation.

Angels do not work miracles; only God can do that, but they can and do give physical assistance. The angels gave physical direction to Philip, to Cornelius, and to Israel in the wilderness. To Elijah, Paul, and Jesus they gave physical sustenance. They gave deliverance to Jacob from Esau, to Daniel from the lions, to Peter and the apostles from prison. They encompass the church at all times (Heb. 12:22). They escort the redeemed to death (Luke 16:22).

In chapter 4 we will look at angels in their capacity as guardians of God's faithful. But first we will devote a chapter to a significant question: Do God's angels actually have bodies?

THREE
THE PHYSICAL NATURE OF SPIRITUAL BEINGS

Do the angels possess bodies? Bible students have been divided over this question for centuries. Augustine, writing in the fifth century, believed that angels possess bodies, though bodies of some ethereal matter. He and some of his contemporaries could not imagine that anything except God could be completely spiritual. But later writings, including the influential Thomas Aquinas, taught that angels are pure intelligences without bodies. Frankly, there is not sufficient evidence in the Bible to make a once-and-for-all pronouncement on the issue.

The Bible does state that when angels appear to humans they are usually in the form of men (see Mark 16:5, for example). To appear as men, they must either assume a human form, or they possess bodies which are real, but spiritual, as was the body of the risen Christ (see Luke 24:39) and as the bodies of risen believers will be (see 1 Cor. 15:39, 46, 50). The characteristics of spiritual bodies (a name that seems to be a contradiction in terms) are demonstrated by Christ, who, after the Resurrection, was able to pass through a closed door (John 20:19) and who was taken up into heaven (Acts 1:10-11), although he also was able to eat real food, and he had marks of his crucifixion (Luke 24:42-43; John 20:27).

The idea of a "spiritual body" is difficult to comprehend. Such an idea has no real parallel in our world, where something is, to us, either physical or spiritual. But it is clear from the passages mentioned above that Christ's resurrected body was somehow both physical *and* spiritual. This means that a resurrected body, a "spiritual body," is freed from the limitations of the original physical body, though it retains characteristics of the original. The spiritual body is something amazing, something on another plane of existence. And many scholars believe that, given the biblical evidence, it is this sort of unusual body that the angels possess.

Certainly the angels do not have "physical" bodies like ours. An angel has a "body," but one such as has not been revealed to us. In 1 Corinthians 15, Paul discusses the bodies of those who are, or shall be, in heaven. He says that there are "celestial bodies" (1 Cor. 15:40). This "spiritual body" (v. 44) is an "incorruptible body; it is a powerful body; it is a glorious body; it is an immortal body." Jesus said that in the resurrection we should be "equal" unto the angels. It also has an "image" — a heavenly image according to Paul, in 1 Corinthians 15:49. These Scriptures help us to understand what is meant by a "spiritual body." Paul says that we should "not be unclothed," but "clothed upon" (2 Cor. 5:4). We shall not be naked, unclothed, super-cosmic spirits, but we shall have bodies of some kind, with all the attributes listed above.

The evidence is clear that when angels bear messages from God to man, they appear to have bodies. In Genesis 18:2, three "men" appeared to Abraham and announced that he would have a son. "They did eat" with him (v. 8) or at least appeared to eat with him. Most Bible scholars believe that one of these men was the Lord, the preincarnate Lord Jesus Christ.

The same type of appearance occurred in Genesis 19:1, where two angels came to Lot at even. They had been sent by the Lord to destroy Sodom and Gomorrah (19:13). They were powerful beings, smiting the men of Sodom with blindness as they attacked the house of Lot (v. 11). To Lot they did not appear as angels, but as lords. They apparently ate with him, talked with him, stayed all night with him, without his realizing fully that they were the messengers of God.

It is not always possible to recognize the divine messengers at the moment that they communicate their message. It was only upon reflection and recall that the momentous fact dawned upon the recipients of the angel's visit. In Gideon's first encounter with the Lord's angel, he does not seem to notice who his visitor is (Judg. 6:11-13). Peter "wist not that it was true which was done by the angel" (Acts 12:9). He thought he had seen "a vision." "And when Peter was come to himself, he said, Now I know of a surety that the Lord hath sent his angel" (Acts 12:11). One recurring feature in the biblical stories is that the people in them only later realize that they have encountered angels. Initially, they believe that mortal men have visited them. Later they seem compelled to admit that something more is involved. They realize that their own small world rests within the wider sphere of the divine. But before this realization occurs, they may find themselves "entertaining angels unawares" (Heb. 13:2).

In other instances, angels look very otherworldly. The seraphim Isaiah saw in the temple have wings (Isa. 6:2), and the living creatures seen by Ezekiel have four faces and four wings (Ezek. 1:6). The cherubim represented on the mercy seat of the ark of the covenant are winged (Exod. 25:18-21), so artists have not been amiss in representing angels as winged creatures. However, in some instances they appear as human beings, but in an exalted state. The angels at Jesus' tomb on Easter morning are dressed in bright shining garments (Luke 24:4; Matt. 28:3; John 20:12). At Jesus' Ascension, two angels in white appear to the disciples (Acts 1:10). Thus, though the Lord's angels can appear as ordinary human beings, they can also appear as glorious and dazzling. When artists show them as powerful, shining, awe-inspiring creatures dressed in beautiful white robes, they are basing their images on Scripture. These images are much more realistic than those of pudgy, winged babies or androgynous youth.

It is interesting that though angels seem to possess bodies of their own, demons — fallen angels — do not. Demons seem to be disembodied spirits who are always passionately seeking a body to inhabit (Matt. 12:45; Mark 5:6-8; Rev. 16:14). This is even more interesting in light of the fact that, though the Bible speaks about the resurrection bodies of believers, the wicked are not mentioned as having bodies. Though demons have the power to perform wonders (Rev. 16:13-14), to communicate with human beings (Matt. 8:31), and to inflict physical infirmities (Matt. 9:32,33; 17:14-18; Mark 5:1-5), they are bodiless creatures who seem to despise the situation of being bodiless, as indicated by the demons inside the Gadarene demoniac, who begged to be sent into swine rather than be sent—without a body to inhabit—to the infernal regions (Luke 8:26-36). Satan and his demons do not seem to function effectively in the world unless they have bodies—preferably human bodies, of course—to possess. It seems that the evil spirits, who only bring pain to the bodies they enter into, envy humans (and even animals) for having bodies. If we agree with tradition that the demons are fallen angels, it is likely that they also envy the holy angels, who still have bodies. And whereas the spiteful demons can only cause pain and destruction to human bodies, the angels, acting out of their love and holiness, can offer protection and guidance to man. In the next chapter we will focus on angels in their role as guardians for believers.

FOUR
THE REALITY OF
GUARDIAN ANGELS

The truth of guardian angels would never have been disputed in the Middle Ages. If one asked a theologian of that time the following questions, they would all have been answered affirmatively:

1. Are there guardian angels?
2. Is a single guardian angel assigned to each individual human being?
3. Are the guardian angels drawn exclusively from the lowest rank of angels?
4. Does every human being have his own guardian angel?
5. Does the angelic guardianship of each human being begin at the moment of birth?
6. Do guardian angels always watch over the individuals they are assigned to guard, never for a moment forsaking their duty in this respect?

Christianity, as mentioned earlier, is not the only religion to believe in angels. Some other world religions have a much more developed angelology. Both Judaism and Islam have many wild superstitions and legends about angels. Only Christianity develops and, through the Holy Spirit, reveals to us a credible account of the personal guardianship of angels. The concept which is so deeply rooted in the very fiber of the human race deserves examination, if not absolute faith.

The belief in guardian angels cannot be lightly brushed aside. Regardless of all the scoffing of atheists, liberal theologians, materialists, humanists, and scorners of all sorts, this belief is going to be with us for a long, long time.

Jesus himself gave credence to the idea that angels serve as guides and guardians of human beings: "Take heed that ye despise not one of these little ones; for I say unto you, that in heaven their angels do always behold the face of my Father which is in heaven" (Matt. 18:10).

Here is the explicit declaration that:

1. There are angels.
2. There are special angels that are assigned to watch people.
3. They are associated with a certain class of people.
4. The certain class is called "little ones."
5. The one despising these angels exposes himself to ruin.

Of whom is Christ speaking here? Is it just of small children? In reading this chapter, Matthew 18, we see that Christ had been attempting to answer a question propounded by His disciples, "Who is the greatest in the kingdom of heaven?" To do this He "called a little child unto him, and set him in the midst of them." He then proceeded to say, "Except ye be converted, and become as little children, ye shall not enter into the kingdom of heaven" (v. 3). Verse 4 follows with the comparison: "Whosoever therefore shall humble himself as this little child, the same is greatest in the kingdom of heaven."

Of this verse the eminent commentator Adam Clarke says two things:

"1. Our Lord here not only alludes to, but in my opinion established the notion received by almost all nations, that every person has a guardian angel; and these have always access to God, to receive orders relative to the management of their charge.
"2. Our Lord's words give us to understand that humble-hearted

childlike disciples are objects of his peculiar care, and constant attention."

In statement No. 1, Dr. Clarke seems to say that every person on earth has a guardian angel. In statement No. 2, however, he seems to limit it to "childlike disciples" who are the "object of his *peculiar care* and *constant attention.*"

John Calvin, another great theologian and commentator on the Scriptures, prefers to think that "not one angel only has the care of *every one of us* but that all the angels together with one consent watch over our salvation." Calvin believed that Christians should be content with the idea that the angels watch over all believers, though there is not necessarily a particular angel assigned to each believer. This may indeed be the case. Whatever the point of view, the one area of agreement is that angels do watch over the faithful.

Angels are not actually assigned to watch over everyone, but only believers. This seems to be properly stated in Hebrews 1:14, where it says that the angels are ministering spirits sent forth to minister to those who are the *heirs of salvation.* At the same time, the angels "rejoice over every sinner that repenteth."

EXPERIENCES WITH THE GUARDIANS

There are many guardian angel experiences that do not yield to any other explanation. The only answer is that a supernatural power intervened. "It must have been a guardian angel," issues from the lips of many an unbeliever. The media abounds with such accounts. The term *guardian angel* is flashed across the TV screen, heard in talk shows, and seen in the newspapers in numberless instances. Perhaps it means that in some future time such an intervention will attain redemptive stature, and the person experiencing it will be led to the Savior.

There is an account in a newspaper before me, in which a plane had its wheels tangled in a 220,000-volt power line and had become trapped like a fly in a spiderweb. The firemen risked their lives to bring the plane down from ninety feet above the ground.

"It was a miracle, a major miracle that we got out alive," one of the fliers said. "I'd like to think that somebody up there was looking out for us." If this is true of nonbelievers, how much more should we as believers give praise to God and acknowledge His holy messengers, the guardian angels.

In the many accounts that I have read or experienced, the work of guardian angels in the life of individuals seems to fall into five categories:

1. A personal appearance of a messenger or deliverer
2. An audible voice
3. An energy take-over
4. A restraining influence
5. A warning

Perhaps many more instances might be adduced, but these seem to be the most prominent categories that illustrate this wonderful experience.

PERSONAL APPEARANCE NO. 1

In his book, *Providential Deliverances,* W. A. Spicer tells of an experience a Christian colporteur had in Norway. In attempting to reach families living in his valley, he had to descend a dangerous mountain trail. At one steep, dangerous place he stopped to pray, asking God to send his angel to go with him. He safely reached the valley. At the first cottage he met a man and his wife, who, it seems, had been watching his descent of the dangerous trail. "What has become of your companion?" "What companion?" asked the missionary. "The man who was with you," they exclaimed in surprise. "We were watching you as you came down the mountain, and it really seemed to us that there were two men crossing the mountain together." "Then," reported missionary Hakland, "I was reminded of my prayer to God for help, and of the word of the Lord in Psalm 34:7: 'The angel of the Lord encampeth round about them that fear him, and delivereth them.' "

PERSONAL APPEARANCE NO. 2

John G. Paton, a missionary to the New Hebrides Islands, tells a thrilling story involving the protective care of angels. Hostile natives surrounded his mission headquarters one night, intent on burning the Patons' hut and killing them. John Paton and his wife prayed all during that terror-filled night that God would deliver them. When daylight came they were amazed to see the attackers unaccountably leave. They thanked God for delivering them. A year later, the chief of the tribe was converted to Jesus Christ, and Paton, remembering what had happened, asked the chief what had kept him and his men from burning down the house and killing them. The chief replied in surprise, "Who were all those men you had with you there?" The missionary answered, "There were no men there — just my wife and me." The chief argued that they had seen many men standing guard — hundreds of big men in shining garments with drawn swords in their hands. They seemed to circle the mission station so that the natives were afraid to attack. Only then did Mr. Paton realize that God had sent His angels to protect them. The chief agreed that there was no other explanation. (This story is told in Billy Graham's book *Angels: God's Secret Agents.*)

PERSONAL APPEARANCE NO. 3

Dr. Graham tells another story in his book. A Persian colporteur was accosted by a man who asked him if he had a right to sell Bibles. "Why, yes," he answered, "we are allowed to sell these books anywhere in the country." The man looked puzzled, and asked, "How is it, then that you are always surrounded by soldiers? I planned three times to attack you, and each time seeing the soldiers, I left you alone. Now I no longer want to harm you."

PERSONAL APPEARANCE NO. 4

Clearly, these illustrations fit in perfectly with the story in 2 Kings 6:15:

"And when the servant of the man of God was risen early, and gone forth, behold, a host compassed the city both with horses and chariots. And his servant said unto him, Alas, my master! how shall we do? And he answered, Fear not: for they that be with us are more than they that be with them. And Elisha prayed, and said, Lord, I pray thee, open his eyes, that he may see. And the Lord opened the eyes of the young man; and he saw: and, behold, the mountain was full of horses and chariots of fire round about Elisha."

There is a veil before our eyes that conceals that invisible world. And there is no army in the world, even the last great army of 200 million, that can compete with the angelic hosts.

AN AUDIBLE VOICE

An account in a recent Sunday school paper tells of a young man on a motorcycle who was saved by a being he felt was a guardian angel.

"The most fantastic, yet inspirational thing that could have happened to me occurred because I wanted to see what the modern-day Sodom and Gomorrah looked like after dark. If I hadn't been so curious, I would never have taken the stupid chance that almost cost me my life. I chose to drive through Las Vegas late at night, when I should have been resting. At dusk I was just coming out of Tonopah, Nevada. I wanted to know what would be so interesting about this town of sin. I knew better. The sensible thing is not to ride through the desert all day in July and then try to ride all night, too. In Nevada the big runoff ditches run at an angle to the highway. They have steep concrete guardrails on the sections in the median strip and run under the traffic lanes. The medians are wide, filled with boulders and clumps of sagebrush. I was beginning to feel wiped out, wondering if I could hold out until I came to a town, but instead of stopping to rest, I kept on. I nodded off, crossed the two lanes of highway, and hit the median strip. I woke up to see the sage and boulders all around and the ditch straight ahead. I bowed my head a second, said, 'Lord, there's nothing I can do,' and grabbed for the hand brake. Suddenly I felt *someone* settle in behind me, and say, 'Keep your hands off the brakes. Relax, I'm taking over.' We angled toward the guardrails. Any one of these boulders or clumps of sage would have wrecked the bike and thrown me over the handlebars. There seemed so little chance I could possibly miss them all, but I did. And straight ahead of me was that concrete ditch rail. We sailed along the edge of the guardrail — my *companion* and I. Then the bike literally shot back onto the road and I took up my place on the freeway. Suddenly I was alone — my *companion* had disappeared as fast as he had come. I don't know where he came from, I don't know where he went. I pulled to the side of the road and got down on my knees. 'Thank you, Lord, for bringing me through this,' I said with bowed head. 'I know my limitations, I'll never exceed them again.' I relearned a lesson that I had known all along. You don't take foolish chances and ride when you are worn out. Really, I learned two lessons. The other: God does care and He does watch out for us. Our guardian angels are real. I felt Him that night, I know. I relive it often."

A RESTRAINING INFLUENCE NO. 1

This unseen power, this hidden energizer, this mysterious strength, was related to me by a truck driver friend. I asked him to relate it for this book:

"It was a foggy, rainy night about eight-thirty. I was en route to Omaha on old Highway 6, about three miles east of Oakland, Iowa. I met three Red Ball trucks. I was driving an eighteen-wheel semi-trailer truck. The generator had not been working for the last one-and-a-half hours, so the headlights were dim. Upon meeting the first truck, mud was splashed on my windshield. I could no longer see the narrow road ahead. By the time I met the second truck I had lost my bearings, and my right wheels dropped off the concrete onto the soft, muddy shoulder, which pulled the truck toward the ditch. Though I desperately struggled to maintain control, the outcome seemed inevitable. I cried, 'Help me, Lord!' Then an unexplainable power changed the course of my momentum. The truck was about to come back on the highway when I encountered a concrete spill-way which was there for the purpose of carrying water from the highway to the ditch. This threw the truck completely out of control, and I was once again headed back to the ditch and a serious accident. Again, I cried, 'O Lord, help me!' This mysterious power again brought the truck back to the concrete highway and under my control. Arriving at Oakland, I had to stop, for my legs were shaking, and I knew that only the Lord's intervention had saved me from a very serious accident. I just praised the Lord and gave Him thanks for I knew the reality of Psalm 34:7: 'The angel of the Lord encampeth round about them that fear him and delivereth them.' In thirty-two years of driving and approximately 3 million miles I was never involved in a serious accident. It was not my personal ability but faith in God as I claimed this verse and received divine help."

A RESTRAINING INFLUENCE NO. 2

Corrie ten Boom relates a story of the angels' restraining influence in her book *A Prisoner and Yet Free.* When Corrie and her sister Betsie arrived as prisoners at the notorious Ravensbruck Prison, all possessions, including clothing, were to be taken from them by the Nazi guards. Relating the horrible indignities and privations they suffered, she writes: "Together we entered the terrifying building. At a table were women who took away all our possessions. Everyone had to undress completely and then go to a room where her hair was clipped short. I asked a guard who was busy checking the possessions of the new arrivals if I might use the toilet. She pointed to a door to the showers. Betsie stayed closed beside me all the time. Suddenly I had an inspiration. 'Quick, take off your woolen underwear,' I whispered to her. I rolled it up with mine and laid the bundle in a corner with my little Bible. The spot was alive with cockroaches, but I didn't worry about that. I felt wonderfully relieved and happy. 'The Lord is busy answering our prayers, Betsie,' I whispered. 'We shall not have to make the sacrifice of all our clothes.'

"We hurried back to a row of women waiting to be undressed. A little later, after we had our showers and put on our shirts and shabby dresses, I hid the roll of underwear and my Bible under my dress. It did bulge out obviously through my dress; but I prayed,

'Lord, cause now thine angels to surround me; and let them not be transparent today for the guards must not see me.' I felt perfectly at ease. Calmly I passed the guards. Everyone was checked, from the front, the sides, the back. Not a bulge escaped the eyes of a guard. The woman just in front of me had hidden a woolen vest under her dress; it was taken from her. They let me pass for they did not see me. Betsie, right behind me, was searched. But outside awaited another danger. On each side of the door were women who looked everyone over for a second time. They felt over the body of each one who passed. I knew they would not see me, for the angels were still surrounding me. I was not even surprised when they passed me by; but within me rose the jubilant cry, 'Lord, if thou dost so answer prayer, I can face even Ravensbruck unafraid.' "

A RESTRAINING INFLUENCE NO. 3

In the book *God's Smuggler* by Brother Andrew we find another such convincing account of the restraining power of angels.

"I spent several days planning my itinerary, scouring Amsterdam for any kind of Christian printed matter in Yugoslav languages, and going over the car for places to conceal what I found. I spent a little time, too, wondering how God was going to supply the money for this trip. The end of March was my target." When Brother Andrew arrived at the Yugoslav border he prayed, " 'Lord, in my luggage is Scripture that I want to take to Your children across the border. When You were on earth You made blind eyes see. Now, I pray, make seeing eyes blind. Do not let the guards see those things You do not want them to see.' When I drove up to the barrier one of the two guards began to examine my camping gear. In the corners and folds of my sleeping bag and tent were boxes of tracts. 'Lord, make these seeing eyes blind.' The other guard was looking inside the VW. . . . He asked me to take out a suitcase. I knew there were tracts scattered through my clothing. 'Of course, sir,' I said. I pulled the front seat forward and dragged the suitcase out. I placed it on the ground and opened the lid. The guard lifted the shirts that lay on top. Beneath, and in plain sight, was a pile of tracts in two different

Yugoslavian languages, Croatian and Slovene. How was God going to handle this situation?

" 'It seems dry for this time of year,' I said to the other guard, and without looking at the fellow who was inspecting the suitcase, I fell into a conversation with him about the weather. I looked behind me. The guard wasn't even glancing at the suitcase. He was listening to our conversation. When I turned around he caught himself and looked up.

" 'Well, then, do you have anything to declare?' 'Only small things,' I said. 'We won't bother with them,' said the guard. He nodded to me that I could close the suitcase, and with a little salute handed me back my passport."

Brother Andrew tells of an even more dramatic action on the part of heaven's emergency service, when he attempted to smuggle Bibles into Romania. "When I pulled up to the checkpoint on the other side of the Danube, I said to myself, 'Well, I'm in luck—only half a dozen cars. They will go swiftly.' When forty minutes had passed and the first car was still being inspected, I thought, 'Poor fellow, they must have something on him to take so long.' But when that car finally left and the next inspection took half an hour too, I began to worry. Literally everything that family was carrying had to be taken out and spread on the ground. Every car in the line was put through the same routine. The guards took the driver inside and kept him there while they removed hubcaps, took his engine apart, removed seats!

" 'Dear Lord,' I said, as at last there was just one car ahead of me, 'What am I going to do? Any serious inspection will show up those Romanian Bibles right away. Lord,' I went on, 'I know that no amount of cleverness on my part can get me through this harder search. Dare I ask for a miracle? Let me take some of the Bibles out and leave them in the open where they can be seen. Then, Lord, I cannot possibly be depending upon my own stratagems, can I? I will be depending utterly upon you.'

"While the last car was going through its chilling inspection, I managed to take several Bibles from their hiding places and pile them on the seat beside me. It was my turn. I put the little VW in low gear, inched up to the officer standing at the left side of the road, handed him my papers, and started to get out. But his knee was against the door, holding it closed. He looked at my photograph on the passport, scribbled something down, shoved the papers back under my nose, and abruptly waved me on. Surely thirty seconds had not passed. I started the engine, and inched forward, my foot above the brake. Nothing happened. I looked in the rearview mirror. The guard was waving the next car to a stop, indicating to the driver that he had to get out. I had made it through that incredible checkpoint in the space of thirty seconds. The guard was *blinded* to Bible literature in plain view."

WARNING THE FAITHFUL

The chief ministry of guardian angels seems to be that of warning. They are represented in Scripture as urging people on. "Get up and get going," the angel said to Peter in the prison. "Get up and get going," the angels said to Elijah. There are some incidents in life which an unbeliever would attribute to luck, even though he was left shaking with fear and wonder. Many believers attribute them to angels.

Under the shadow of the horror of Hiroshima emerges a story of the ministry of guardian angels that is unparalleled. The dramatic escape that was related in my hearing is a startling proof that guardian angels minister just as they did in biblical times.

It was my good fortune to meet the principals in this account in an unexpected gathering one evening in Tokyo. I came to know them when I was speaking at Tokyo's seminary, part of an evangelistic tour of the Orient. A tea had been arranged for us in one of the rooms adjacent to the seminary auditorium. These people were brought together without any previous planning. It was intended to be only a social gathering. The result was a memorable and convincing testimony to the intervention in the human arena by supernatural forces.

The story that I heard from the lips of witnesses that night in Japan should challenge the most skeptical. Two angels once walked the streets of doomed Sodom, seeking an endangered family. Three people of Sodom were destined to escape one of the most awful cataclysms the world has ever known. The deliverance of Lot was to remain forever a convincing testimony that there are angels sent by God to deliver his children (2 Pet. 2:9). The parallels of the account narrated by Mutsuko Hasegawa and the story of Sodom could be extended to great length.

Included in our group that night was Jacob DeShazer, the former bombardier who became a Christian missionary. Also in the group was his former enemy, a submarine captain, Mr. Hasegawa, formerly Mr. Yokota. Hasegawa was now a brother in Christ. I shall never forget the stunned expression on DeShazer's face as he was introduced to Hasegawa. He hesitated briefly, then rushed toward him and threw his arms around him in a warm embrace of love. DeShazer said, "If I had found you out there years ago, I would have sent you to the bottom of the ocean." Thirty years after the war, enemies were brothers.

Hasegawa had married Mutsuko Hasegawa and had taken her name. The central actress in this drama, Mutsuko Hasegawa, had been brought to know the Lord Jesus Christ through the effort of a young American missionary, Miss Mabel Francis. Mutsuko was the young daughter of a town mayor in Hiroshima. She had social standing and financial security, but she felt that Jesus was calling her to be a missionary like Miss Francis. However, in her case such a desire was effectively blocked. It was not her independent decision. Mutsuko learned instead that her parents had already arranged a marriage for her with a non-Christian man. All protests were unavailing, she was disconsolate, but family counsel and custom prevailed.

She was eventually assured in her heart that even in this the Lord could work out all things together for good. The years passed, and three little girls were born—Yasuko, Tadko, and Naoko. All seemed to be going well, when one day the mother was called to bring her three children and to appear at the municipal office. There she learned that her husband had died for the emperor in World War II. Although multitudes were being sacrificed on the altar of Japanese greed for conquest, yet she never had dreamed that it could happen to her!

Suicide is the common way out for frustrated Japanese. On the way back to Hiroshima, as they crossed the high trestle, she resolved to push the three girls out, and then she would follow them to destruction. How could she support, protect, and raise three little girls in Japanese society? She would open the door, jump out, and that would be the end of her trouble.

Suddenly through Mutsuko's mind flashed a thought which she recognized to be a supernatural voice. It said, "You wanted to be a missionary, didn't you? Can't you train these girls to be missionaries for me?" She was transported by the voice in her soul from the darkness of despair to the light of a glorious hope for the future. She asked the Lord to forgive her for unbelief, and for the resolution that she had made to quench the light of four precious lives, destined for God's service.

As she came back to Hiroshima, things began to change for the better. Her doctor sister-in-law employed her as a dietitian in her clinic. Life began to seem good once more in the beautiful city of Hiroshima.

Yet in the midst of much improved circumstances, there came a maddening voice, a persistent, unexplainable voice: "Escape to the mountain, escape to the mountain." For several months she had shared the warning with her friends, but they pleaded with her to remain.

"Why," they reasoned, "should they bomb us?" True, Tokyo had been leveled and burned, but the B-29s that had razed it and Nagoya and other populous cities had passed right over them. They thought that Hiroshima contained no military objectives.

Japan was preparing for a last stand. They expected to lose millions in the dreaded invasion. Although there was a shortage of weapons, even women and children were being taught to fight with the most primitive of weapons. There were five thousand suicide bombers hidden around Hiroshima. It was the communications center for the defense of Kyushu, and it was expected the invasion would first hit on this island. They were correct in their intelligence — this was planned by the Americans as the objective. They never thought that the Americans would bomb their prisoners of war, a number of whom were incarcerated there. So the huge Mr.

BeSans continued to drone over the lovely city sleeping in the sun, as only the ominous shadow of B-29's appeared almost hourly over the doomed city and quickly disappeared.

Mutsuko's doctor sister-in-law told her that if a higher salary would be required it would be forthcoming. Whatever else was needed could be arranged. She stayed for a while, but still the insistent words were ringing more and more urgently: "Escape to the mountain, escape to the mountain!" Finally, although she could not rationalize the strange warning, she knew that it was a divine voice which spoke to her. She told the sister-in-law that a supernatural voice was telling her to leave. The sister-in-law readily agreed and said that if it were God who ordered her thus she must obey. She gathered up her goods, and, rather dazed, packed all her earthly possessions into a hired lorry. Then she gathered her three children for the hard trip out of the city, leaving security and love behind in order to follow the voice of her Lord. Nothing less than the constant pounding of her inner consciousness and her desire to follow God could have ever persuaded her to leave lovely Hiroshima behind. All that she needed had been provided by the Lord since the death of her husband.

At 8:16 the very next morning came the blinding flash, the shock wave rolling even up to the hills and beyond, the awesome mushroom cloud, the searing heat. Like Lot of old, who was pulled out of Sodom and viewed the awful judgment from the mountains, Mutsuko viewed the death of Hiroshima from the far-off hills. Divine protection had led her and three little potential missionaries to safety and service for His kingdom.

I myself have experienced the ministry of guardian angels many times. I relate some of them now in the following chapters, for I hope to share with you stories of God's divine care in all circumstances.

48

PART TWO
My Encounters with Angels

FIVE
ANGEL IN THE PASTURE

God still sustains and strengthens those he loves. In my many years of travel I have been constantly reminded of how He protects us. How can I praise God adequately, for in countless trips at home and abroad He has preserved me from any loss of passports, money, or documents. I do not attribute this to my own vigilance, but only to God's angels.

Eddie Rickenbacker, the famous World War I flying ace, told Lowell Thomas that he had had brushes with death 134 times. He had numerous wrecks, but seemed to have a charmed life. Once he floated in the Pacific Ocean twenty-four days. His last escape as the result of an airliner crash in the Atlantic Ocean left him more dead than alive. "I've cheated the Grim Reaper more times than anyone I know," he said. He lived to be eighty-two years of age. Eddie believed emphatically in the old-fashioned virtues — thrift, hard work, love of country, and belief in God. Morning and night he got down on his knees to pray. Once he said, "My angels were always hovering over me."

I feel that I too have had a "charmed life." When a lad of about twelve, after the death of my mother, I gravitated back and forth between my home in the city and my grandfather's farm. I loved the farm and went there at every opportunity. I had several cousins near my own age who lived about a half mile away. We grew up together.

51

The two boys and I were mischievous like all boys of our age. My uncle lived on another farm south of us and owned a large herd of cattle, which was supervised by a large bull by the name of Gunderson. (The origin of the name was cloaked in mystery.) Gunderson was a powerfully built animal and very dangerous. He was a fighting bull, bred for the bull ring, it might seem, and the very sight of us boys seemed to enrage him. With a matador to challenge and wave his red cape before him, with a picador to jab home the banderillas in his broad shoulders, he would have enraptured any crowd with his furious charges. We boys liked to goad him into a frenzy in various ways, although we always kept a safe distance away. It was always my fear that I would someday meet him and he would exact the penalty for the torment we had inflicted upon him.

On one particular day my grandmother wanted me to carry a washboard down to my aunt. I wanted to go around by the road, rather than through the pastures, because I was afraid this great animal might be with the cows. My grandmother was in a hurry, and she insisted that I go directly through the pastures to my aunt's place. I obeyed reluctantly, and I ran a small rope through the top of the washboard so that I could carry it around my neck instead of in my hands. It flapped back and forth on my back as I walked through the dreaded paths to my uncle's farm. As I passed down through the familiar glades, I had a haunting fear that something was wrong, but because of my grandmother's insistence I did not dare to turn back. I had to pass through two gates, one of which was the first boundary line, and then through another that I knew would let me through to my uncle's farm.

As I got close to the last gate, I heard the tinkling of cowbells, and I knew that the herd was right ahead of me. In fact, it was feeding right between me and the gate through which I hoped to pass to safety. I did not know where Gunderson was, but if he were anywhere near, I planned a quick dive under the barbed wire gate to safety. I carefully pushed the screen of leaves aside, preparing to take my slide. There was only a thin screen of brush between me and the cows. I carefully pushed the screen of leaves aside, ready to spring, and there looking savagely at me was Gunderson. I was staring into the red eyes of this monster from less than ten feet away! He was the incarnation of fury when he saw me. I was petrified momentarily as I looked into the blazing eyes. Head lowered, he studied me. We both hesitated to make a move. I could not turn back — he would have trampled me to death. He had no horns, but he had an enormous head which could have butted me to death with ease. The spell broke — I knew I had to act. I gave a yell and turned sharply to the right, running along parallel to the barbed wire fence. I hardly knew where I was going, but I knew I was running for my life. Gunderson let out a roar, and ran bellowing after me as I ran along the fence looking for a gate, but in vain. I could hear the thunder of his hooves behind me — his breath was almost literally on the back of my neck. All the time the old washboard was flapping up and down on my back, held by the rope under my chin.

I was never a runner, much less a hurdler. I have only one answer for the inspiration that came to me at that terrible moment; I know it was from an ever-present guardian angel. I had never *jumped* a fence in my life, but I knew I had to jump this one. I had no time to weigh the problem — death was right behind me. You can call it what you will — a shot of adrenaline, strength to do the impossible, whatever. I accept none of those explanations. They are totally inadequate. There was not enough spring in my legs to lift me over that high barbed wire in an instant. Suddenly, however, something lifted me clear up, and I flew over the fence like a bird. As I went over, the washboard caught on the top of the wire, hooked under my chin, and dumped me flat on my back inches on the other side. There I lay, with only a fragile barbed wire fence between me and a roaring, red-eyed bull, pawing the dirt in fury. While I was lying there, the dog ran up and chased the furious animal back to the cows. I picked myself up, thankful to be delivered from sure death as other members of my uncle's family ran up to help me. What was the energy that at that moment wafted me right over that top wire? It was a guardian angel.

SIX
ANGEL AS A LIFEGUARD

In 1921, on a hot Sunday afternoon in Minnesota, I went swimming against my father's orders. He was a very strict member of our church and had forbidden this sport on Sunday, but the cool waters of Rice Lake lured me on to ignore his explicit commands. All winter the lake had been frozen over. Now on this late spring day, the broken fragments of a wooden pier, shattered by melting ice, were floating about. Like many other teenagers, I took a chance. I was not able to swim, but waded out and sat on one of the floating sections of the pier, slowly drifting farther and farther from the shore. I was laughing and engaging in horseplay with some friends when the pier tipped and I plunged into the water.

I felt no fear as I fell into the water, as I expected to easily grasp the pier on rising to the surface. However, it had drifted beyond my reach, and as water filled my eyes, I could not see it. I sank again. Like any nonswimmer I panicked and started to thrash around, rising to the surface again. I yelled for help, sank again, my lungs filling with water. I remember vividly what were nearly my last moments on earth. I felt myself slowly sinking into unconsciousness and, surprisingly, my only thought was, "I will never be able to go to school again!" This thought spurred me to a desperate struggle, but it was futile, as I sank into the weeds on the bottom of the lake, all hope gone.

The next moments were the turning point of my young life. These are the facts as I learned them from observers: A gentleman *happened* to be on shore. He struck out for me with great speed, pulled me up on the shore, and vanished. All I can remember was having a splitting headache and realizing the fact that I was alive.

I never had the chance to thank my unknown savior for deliverance from certain death. I was plucked from a watery grave as surely as John Wesley was delivered from the flames of Epworth parsonage. How did this powerful swimmer happen to be there at that exact instant? The unbeliever in angels would say, "accident." I say, "angel." My heart overflows with gratitude to God and to my unknown deliverer.

My daughters say: "Dad, you have a guardian angel." I do not argue with them. I can only agree with their opinion. I do not attempt to rationalize a clear assurance from Jesus Christ. He said, "In heaven their angels do always behold the face of my Father which is in heaven." As a believer, I claim that promise in a very special way. I rejoice that I have such an angelic companion. And so have you, if you are one of his little ones. A guardian angel was there that day, and in numberless experiences, some of which I shall relate in this book. I would have died that day, but for an angel. With great thanksgiving I testify with the Psalmist, who wrote, "He sent from above, he took me, he drew me out of many waters" (Ps. 18:16).

SEVEN
ANGELS AND AIRPLANES

After I discovered the airplane as a mode of travel (that is, after I had graduated from riding on the decaying railroad system of this country), I was engaged with my church work in traveling about 200,000 miles a year. Mounting and dismounting from planes became so common that I often found myself becoming a little careless, or so absorbed in my work that I did not always carefully identify the plane on which I was to ride or check my boarding pass or ticket. Yet I can say that in all those millions of miles, I was never taken to the wrong destination.

A remarkable instance of this occurred once while boarding a plane in Oklahoma City. My destination was Chicago, and from there to Winona Lake, Indiana, where my denomination's headquarters are located. I went through the regular airport procedures and rather absentmindedly boarded a plane that was sitting out near the exit from the departure lounge. I was very tired, and as was my usual custom, I settled down for a good rest. The plane started up and was rolling down the runway at its increasingly high rate of speed, increasing all the time. Suddenly I heard over the intercom the disturbing announcement: "You are now on flight No. — — heading for Denver, Colorado." I shot up off my seat. I was on the wrong plane, going in the opposite direction. At that moment the flight attendant was hurrying down the aisle in the usual fashion. I grabbed her arm, "I'm on the wrong plane, I am supposed to be going to Chicago!"

This seems unbelievable, but when the flight attendant rushed up and informed the pilot, he stopped the plane, which was about to leave the ground traveling at great speed. He wheeled the giant bird around, came back to the airport, let me off, and took off again! I doubt if such an experience has been duplicated in the history of air travel! (This the reader will probably find it hard to believe. I wonder if it has ever happened to anyone before. That I was saved from a serious disruption of my schedule is only because of the ministry of angels.)

This incident is highly unusual, because in other instances I had never succeeded in making any such change in the pilots' plans. I recall that on a trip to Ireland our plane was delayed in Seattle about two hours. I was supposed to connect with a British Airways plane in Chicago that was on a matching time with my arrival. I rushed furiously through the terminal and got out on the runway and stood right at the door of the British Airways plane, which had just been closed. Despite all my pleas, they refused to open the door and admit me. I missed my connection as a result, and I had to wait overnight in New York. The next day I went on one of the most rickety, uncomfortable planes I have ever ridden. When I arrived in London, all my arrangements were disrupted, including my hotel arrangements. But the incident related above was totally different.

I have had many other experiences involving the ministry of angels while traveling by plane. I have often been conscious of a sudden uplift in my spirits in time of crisis. While taking a trip from Berlin to Rome, I was traveling with a man who had been an experienced pilot for many years, and he was thoroughly acquainted with operational procedures. He had regaled me on the trip with some of his experiences and had me convinced that he was equal to most any crisis that we might possibly encounter. We did not expect to encounter any on this flight. Our plane was a four-engine Electra 188, one of a new breed of turboprop machines that were a vast improvement over the old DC3s and DC6s. It excelled them greatly in smoothness and speed. I did not know at the time, however, that a fatal weakness was to be found inherent in this new beauty of the skies. The Electra was the toast of the pilots when it was introduced, but from 1959 to 1985 there were twelve fatal crashes, with a total of 507 people who perished. Out of the one hundred and seventy planes produced, thirty-nine crashed.

I was on an Electra, but of course, knew nothing of these problems. Its smoothness, maneuverability, and comfort were delightful. We had flown from Frankfurt, Germany, to the summit of the Alps. Our first stop was at Milan, just on the southern side of the Alps. Mountain peaks were all around us, a glorious panorama. The seat-belt sign came on, and we were instructed to prepare to land at Milan airport.

At that moment a storm hit us with devastating force. We plummeted down and then shot up like a chip on an ocean wave. Outside the sky turned almost black, and one could hardly see the wingtips. How quickly the atmosphere in a plane can change when disaster threatens! (I recall Dr. Billy Graham telling about sitting in a plane next to an apparently very wealthy man. Billy began to approach him about his relationship to Jesus Christ, but the man very rudely turned him off. Just about then the plane took a dive and began to shake all over in vicious air turbulence. The man turned to Billy and said, "Just what was that you were saying a little while ago, Rev.?")

I glanced at my friend and noticed that he was pale. Looking out of the opposite window, I noticed the wings silhouetted against the black sky. They were weaving in the tremendous turbulence, actually flapping in the powerful air currents. We were the playthings of the storm. The pilots were trying to keep the plane in the racecourse pattern, well-known to air travelers. In the light of the information I have so recently read about the Electra I wonder what prevented those wildly waving wings from snapping off. I am convinced only some other power kept them intact.

The atmosphere of the plane was traumatized by the awful shaking and vibrating. I looked at my friend, who was getting paler as he looked out the window. The woman next to me, evidently a Catholic, was counting her rosary beads and moaning. People were getting out of their seats and running up and down the aisles. The flight attendants were dashing up and down the aisles trying to calm the passengers and place them back in their seats. Panic had taken over — the plane was helplessly driven by the storm. I knew that at any moment, a drop in altitude would plunge us into an Alpine mountain peak.

Yet in this deadly peril I felt a strange peace. I looked at my friend again. Perspiration was rolling down his face, standing on his upper lip. Out of the storm had roared a sheet of hail. It sounded like a battery of machine gun bullets was strafing us. All around were the moans and the screams of the passengers. "Look," my friend said, "his ailerons are freezing up — the exhausts are full of ice." Yet this did not seem to alarm me in the least, that the pilot might lose control completely. That strange composure still filled my heart — a wonderful, inexhaustible peace. After what seemed an eternity, a patch of green appeared in the clouds — I could see the ground. Soon, we were plunging down through the torrential sheets of rain to a rough, but safe landing. I cannot call this anything less than the ministry of angels. "Fear thou not; for I am with thee; be not dismayed; for I am thy God; I will strengthen thee; yea, I will help thee; yea, I will uphold thee with the right hand of my righteousness" (Isa. 41:10). "I will uphold thee;" how literally this promise was fulfilled.

EIGHT
AN ANGEL SPOKE STERNLY

Sometimes we must speak sternly to our children. It is especially so when we see them facing some grave danger. This was my experience in 1928 when I was a desk clerk at the Seattle Central YMCA. An angel spoke and turned my life around — but he spoke sternly.

A number of us Seattle Pacific College students owe a debt of undying gratitude to the YMCA. We always lived at the poverty level, it seemed, while attempting to work our way through college. Employment at the "Y," however, greatly enhanced our life-style and gave us much greater freedom in pursuing our college career.

The Young Men's Christian Association was an outstanding Christian institution. The leaders were devoted men of God. Arn Allen, George Fuller, and others were earnestly striving to maintain the "C" in the name of the YMCA. The atmosphere was wholesome and healthy, and people were like real brothers. After a year at the Seaman's YMCA on the waterfront, I graduated to the uptown YMCA. The pay was seventy-five dollars a month, quite a sum in those days. After our graduation my wife worked in the cafeteria. We had a cozy little apartment near the college. I played golf every morning after working all night. Life was full to the brim with enjoyment. I felt smugly content and went about fulfilling my religious obligations by teaching a class in one of the churches in the city.

Life at night in the YMCA was sometimes quite eventful. We were on the verge of the Depression, unemployment was high, and holdups were frequent. One night I heard repeated shots out on the street. I rushed out to find Joe, the man who ran a hamburger stand across the street, covered with blood. He had gone berserk when two men had come in and held him up. He had shot at them, and they had shot back.

About that same time I was working the night shift when a couple of fellows walked into the lobby. Suddenly they vaulted over the counter, guns in hand. One man jammed his gun into my stomach and threatened to shoot me. I was terrified. I didn't know what the combination to the safe was, and I knew that was what they wanted. But to my immense relief, they only wanted the money in the till. They left after taking the cash in the till, but they were picked up by the police soon after, and I was called in to identify them.

So life at the YMCA was both thrilling and placid at times. I had decided that I would become a part of the YMCA and make it my career. I never expected to be anything other than a YMCA administrator.

I must confess that from my earliest childhood I had had a vague feeling that I might be a preacher. Public speaking came easily to me, and I was constantly called on to participate in platform programs of various kinds all through my academic life. But there had never been a real, deliberate *call*. So I had let my college years slide by without any deliberate preparation for ministry. I had taken some language courses to prepare myself for archaeological work, but had done no real study for Christian work. However, I found, as I have found many times, that God and His angels lead us into what is both unexpected and glorious.

One sunny day I was working at the counter of the YMCA at my usual task. I had given very little thought to preaching, if any, at this time in my life. My whole life was now oriented to being a successful YMCA executive. After all, what could be better Christian work?

Then, on that bright, sunny day, it hit me like a bolt of lightning out of the heavens. A stern voice spoke peremptorily to me, "Are you going to preach my gospel or are you going to hell?" I was shaken to the very depths of my being. I had heard that voice before. There was no clear balancing of alternatives — there was only one. I was utterly unprepared for this supreme question — my life's pattern had been set for some time.

Immediately another angel spoke — that dark angel, Satan. He said very clearly, "You know what this means, don't you? No more fun, no more social life. You will have a constant struggle for survival. You will have a dull drab existence." He recalled to me the little white churches of my childhood. As in a vision of the past I saw again the old churches and parsonages, especially the rural ones with no young people.

I did not struggle long with my great enemy. I had to admit that he was probably telling me the truth for once. "How do you like it?" he sneered. I was as in a dream. I do not know what anyone thought as I stood there behind the desk, watching all my dreams being threatened now by a guardian angel. I must have appeared as if mesmerized, as I was swayed by the forces of heaven on the one hand and the forces of darkness on the other.

"I don't like it," I replied to Satan, "but I don't want to go to hell, either." A pretty poor incentive, someone might object, but perhaps a little "hell-scare" might help some to make the right decision! Without another moment's hesitation, I folded up my book, left my desk, and appeared at the office of the general secretary. I told him of my decision. He was astounded. He said, "Why, Northrup, I thought you were going to devote your life to being a YMCA secretary." "I did, too," I firmly replied, "until a few minutes ago, but my mind has been changed."

I walked out of the YMCA sadly, but forever. My wife and I evacuated our little apartment and loaded all our worldly goods into a little Model T roadster. We went to our first, difficult appointment. Satan was such a liar, as always. Nearly sixty years of ministry have proved to be the most glorious, rewarding, and joyful period of our lives.

In one moment, a guardian angel turned my whole life around. God can speak to you as clearly as He did to me. Guardianship means guidance. God sent an angel to arrest me. His love now holds me forever.

NINE
ANGEL IN LEBANON

Lebanon — it writhes in agony with the rattle of machine guns and the moaning of the innocents caught in the deadly cross fire. The broken bodies being tenderly carried from the rubble of bombed-out embassies move across our TV screen, mirroring the agony of a most beautiful land.

Lebanon was once one of the most delightful countries of the Middle East. From the delightfully blue waters of the Mediterranean to the Hama Valley and the Shouf Mountains it was lovely and restful. Its beautiful coastline, washed by the sea for millennia, has fantastic grottoes. The wealthy relax in soaring condominiums perched on the cliffs overlooking the sea and loll on its glorious beaches, seemingly immune to the battles roaring not far away.

This beautiful land also has a rich history. Although only as large as the state of New Jersey, it has seen some of the greatest movements of the ages. Lebanon is the land of the great Hittite race, the people who once dominated the Mediterranean basin. I saw on the wall of our hotel a picture of the graceful Hittite ships with their sweeping curves, strikingly similar to the Viking ships which once plied the Atlantic. From the forests of this ancient land, Hiram of Tyre floated on the Litani River the huge cedar trees used in building Solomon's temple and palace. Today only a few of these majestic trees remain on the mountains of Lebanon.

Today Beirut is a nightmare of destruction. The city is divided into warring sectors where death rides on the waves of agelong religious and political strife. This is a shame, for Beirut was once, not long ago, one of the most sophisticated and alluring cities in the Middle East. There the ancient and the modern met in splendor. The old city still contains the remains of the great Hittite civilization. The ruins awe the beholder. Art, commerce, and sophisticated elegance made Beirut an attractive stop for travelers. Today no tour group would risk its people in Lebanon.

One of the chief attractions of Lebanon was and is the ancient city of Baalbek. In Baalbek is the most colossal temple complex ever erected by man. Augustus Caesar resolved to build there the greatest temple on earth. He succeeded grandly.

I left Beirut through the Dog River Canyon on the way to Damascus, Syria. Through the fertile Hama Valley where peasants were tilling the land with ancient tools we came to Baalbek where Egyptians, Babylonians, Greeks, Romans, Crusaders, French, and Turks had all passed and helped to shatter its noble buildings. Then in 1812 a great earthquake had tumbled down most of the pillars of the huge temple complex.

The gigantic proportions of Baalbek's temple awe the traveler. Here remain only six great pillars crowned with stupendous capitals. Once there were 154 granite shafts around the vast temple enclosure. They were of solid granite transported from Aswan in Upper Egypt. These enormous pillars — about seventy feet high — are each composed of one solid block. How these were quarried, floated down the Nile, shipped across the Mediterranean, and erected in Lebanon boggles the mind. One also wonders how the magnificent capitals were placed atop the pillars. One of the capitals, the famous Lion Capital, has fallen to the ground and remains upright. It is taller than a man and is elaborately carved. The engineering and artistic skills of these people must have been amazing.

Outside of Baalbek lies what is called the "Sleeping Pillar of Baalbek." It weighs a thousand tons. For some reason it was never erected but abandoned by the builders. I climbed up on it to be photographed, and standing on this fallen giant I seemed no larger than a fly.

After spending considerable time inspecting the vast ruins, with my camera in hand I had climbed up on a very high wall adjacent to the temple to get a better angle for my final picture. It was to be my last picture before leaving, and, not having a wide-angle lens at that time, I wanted to get the entire temple area into one single frame. This required that I be quite a distance away and demanded especially great height. In my breathless excitement, gazing over the vast ruin, I was backing into a position that could plunge me to destruction below! Suddenly, I felt a distinct pressure on my back. I was held there by an unseen hand. I could not step back another inch. It was as if I were against an invisible wall.

Held there by this unseen force, I carefully turned my head and looked over my shoulder without moving my body. Imagine my horror when I found that I was nearly a hundred feet above the ground and right on the brink of falling to certain death. Yet I could not move. I was momentarily transfixed to the spot. With my body covered with perspiration, still held by this heavenly hand, I was carefully guided down to safety. I had almost taken my last picture ever — had it not been for the intervention of a guardian angel. That unseen heavenly angel in all my travels had kept me from yet another fatal calamity.

The words of the psalmist were true for me: "Thou hast beset me behind and before, and laid thine hand upon me" (Ps. 139:5). Could anything be more clear? It was the same angel of whom he wrote in another place, "For he shall give his angels charge over thee, to keep thee in all thy ways. They shall bear thee up in their hands, lest thou dash thy foot against a stone" (Ps. 91:11-12). I cannot explain it, but I can join David in saying, "How precious also are thy thoughts unto me, O God! how great is the sum of them! If I should count them, they are more in number than the sand: when I awake, I am still with thee" (Ps. 139:17-18).

TEN
ANGEL IN DARKNESS UNDER THE DOME OF THE ROCK

I was in Mammoth Cave in Kentucky. The guide said, "We will now turn off the lights and you will be in total darkness." You may have never been in total darkness before, where there is an absolute absence of any light. When the lights went off we could almost feel the darkness with our hands, like black velvet. What a relief as the lights came on once more. Years later I faced a somewhat similar experience, except I had no guide, and no lights to turn on. This happened in a city I have visited many times, Jerusalem.

I have often been asked, "What is the most beautiful building you have seen in all your travels?" I always reply, without hesitation, "The Taj Mahal." When I first saw the Taj Mahal, I thought I must have been dreaming. It seemed to be suspended in the atmosphere, swimming in a mist of glory. But next to the Taj Mahal, I acclaim as the most beautiful building the Haram es Sharif, the Dome of the Rock in Jerusalem. This jewel has survived the attrition of twelve centuries to still glow with its ancient beauty. It has captivated me for twenty years, as I return again and again to its magnificent portals. Under the gloriously blue sky of Jerusalem, framed by its delicate arches, gleaming with dazzling tile, it is a photographer's dream. It is irresistible. Its golden dome magnetizes me, as it does everyone, dominating the skyline of the Holy City. The nearer you drive toward it, the more it overawes you with its grandeur.

It is hard to believe that this shrine covers an area which was once considered the "garbage dump" of Jerusalem. The area was for many years despised by Jerusalem Christians because the Jewish temple once stood there. When Omar, the first Arab conqueror of Jerusalem, took over in the year 637, he angrily compelled Patriarch Sophronius and his fellow Christians to carry away with their own hands the accumulated debris in the area. The Muslims considered the area holy, and they hated the Christians because, in Muslim eyes, they had desecrated the holy spot.

On the site Omar raised a wooden mosque which could accommodate three thousand worshipers. In 691 Caliph Abdul Malik realized that too much of his potential revenue was being lost through the traffic of pilgrims to Mecca, the Muslim holy city in Arabia. Abdul Malik built the present glorious structure to attract the pilgrims who did not want to go so far as Mecca. He was enormously successful, for pilgrims were drawn to the magnificent building. The great dome was covered with gold plate. A Persian traveler described it as "a blazing dome that can be seen from the distance of a league away, rising like the summit of a mountain." That view is still available to visitors to Jerusalem. And visitors still marvel at the gorgeous Turkish tile on the walls. Much restoration work has been done in this century, and the Dome of the Rock continues to dazzle human eyes. Next to Mecca and Medina, it is the holiest spot in Islam. It is also a place where religious and political tensions are always present, and, as I will relate in a later chapter, much fighting still occurs on this beautiful but troubled spot.

The story that is the focus of this chapter concerns a lesser known part of this area. When Herod the Great envisioned his great temple in the years between 40 and 6 B.C., he enlarged the temple area from seventeen acres to the present thirty-six acres. The ground sloped off sharply just to the south of the temple area. He made an enormous fill and stretched out the huge platform over an amazing substructure erroneously called "Solomon's Stables." This great substructure consists of a labyrinth of pillars which support the southern end of the huge platform. There are rows of altogether eighty-eight pillars forming thirteen galleries. Their extent from east to west is twenty-seven feet, and from north to south it is 198 feet.

During the Crusades this area was used for stables by the Knights Templars.

Today this underground area is relatively unknown to the general public. I have never seen it advertised in a tour brochure as something to be visited in Jerusalem. Many people have speculated about what wonders might lie in this area. Some have claimed that the ark of the covenant might be there.

In 1969 I resolved to visit the mysterious "Solomon's Stables." One bright day I found the Arab doorkeeper sitting in the sun at the entrance to the stairway leading down under the great Dome platform. He readily admitted me to the vast enclosure. I was the only person down there, and I admit I was somewhat apprehensive as I advanced toward the labyrinth of columns. A narrow shaft of light was shining through a tiny window in the wall on the Kidron Valley side. This was the only illumination, and I was moving farther and farther away from it into the darkness. The shadowy pillars seemed to melt away in the distance. I thought, "What would happen if the Arab would go away, lock the door, and leave me here?" I could envision myself totally lost among those endless rows of arches and pillars.

I was aware also of another real danger; on the other side of the city there is what is known as the "quarries of Solomon." One entered these quarries under the northern wall not far from the Damascus Gate. They, unlike the area under the Dome platform, were lighted dimly, and you paid a price for admission. They were fairly frequently visited by the public. I went in there at one time, but vividly remember getting out so far that I could not see the dim light bulbs, and also I thought there yawned before me some very deep pits in the floor. I retreated rather hastily, and never did fully explore them. The quarries run southward for about 550 feet in a direct line with Solomon's Stables. It is thought that the tremendous stones for Solomon's temple were quarried here. The biblical account tells that the stones for the temple were prepared in the quarry, and that "there was neither hammer nor axe nor any tool of iron heard in the house while it was in building" (1 Kings 6:7). I thought as I walked through the pillars in the stables, "How much farther will I go before I reach these vast caves of the quarry, and perhaps fall into one of them?" My devouring curiosity kept me going farther, however, into the darkness.

Suddenly I had a distinct impression. It was as if I were confronted by a mysterious presence. The presence warned me, "Go no farther." It was so peremptory and commanding that I stopped immediately. I knew it could not have originated in my psyche. It was not the logical result of my thinking about the danger. I knew, then, that it was an angel. I stopped, turned around, and felt my way along through the pillars, guided only by the faint shaft of light from the window in the ancient wall. I climbed the stairs and the Arab doorkeeper opened to me. I stumbled out into the bright sunlight, rejoicing that I had been delivered from what could have been easily a disastrous experience, had it not been for my watchful angel.

I lingered for a little while, recovering from my walk through the pillars, and taking some more pictures of the brilliantly lighted scene in the square. It seemed doubly glorious after the darkness below.

A few minutes later two young men arrived and asked for admittance. The Arab opened the door for them, and not long after that he arose and started off for his siesta. Before he left, he locked the door. He was almost out of sight across the huge square when I heard a terrific pounding and yelling at the door leading to the area above. The two fellows had lingered too long. I realized their desperate plight. I ran after the doorkeeper and implored him to return. Life is cheap in Arab countries, and it took a little persuading, as the yelling and pounding mounted in a rising crescendo. The Arab unlocked the door and they, too, stumbled out into the light, much to my relief and their joy.

That vivid experience made me ponder, "That could have been me at the locked door—with no one to run after the doorkeeper and let me out." The strange warning I knew was from a guardian angel. It was that strange presence which so effectively blocked my way.

ELEVEN
BLOND ANGEL IN JERUSALEM

Israel, land of the Bible, is the oldest country of pilgrimage, and the only one to draw pilgrims of three faiths. To some, a pilgrimage to Israel is the goal of a lifetime. To those who are willing to sacrifice any amount of time or money to achieve the opportunity to follow the sacred paths trodden by their Savior, a pilgrimage to the Holy Land can be a life-changing experience.

The two people who did the most to make Palestine a center of pilgrimage were Constantine the Great and his mother, Helena, both converts from paganism. At the Council of Nicea in the year 325, Constantine heard a council delegate from Palestine claim that nothing had been done to preserve and commemorate the sites where the last events of Jesus' earthly life took place. Jerusalem was in deplorable condition. In 135 Emperor Hadrian, enraged because of a Jewish rebellion, had razed Jerusalem to the ground. He had erected a huge temple to Venus to show the triumph of paganism. He had also erected a huge equestrian statue of himself to show the might of imperial Rome. At the time of Constantine, the statue of Hadrian was still standing.

Helena was greatly moved by the report on Palestine. A year later, in 326, she traveled to Palestine. When she returned she claimed to have located most of the holy sites connected with the life of Jesus, and she inaugurated a pilgrimage movement that has never ceased. Constantine opened up the coffers of his large empire and embarked on a plan of building churches on the holy sites. On the hill they assumed was Calvary, Constantine erected a church that was supposed to surpass every church in the world. The church became the focus of Christian pilgrimage. Over the centuries devout believers made their way to the Holy Land. They still do, and even though the trip is much less grueling than it was in the Middle Ages, it can still be exhausting, especially if the pilgrim arrives at one of the most crowded of times, Easter.

The Greek Orthodox celebration of Holy Week is magnificent. (It should be mentioned that the Orthodox churches, which use the old Julian calendar, celebrate Easter on a Sunday different from Catholics and Protestants.) The climax of the celebration of Easter is on Easter Saturday. At that time the "Holy Fire" is supposed to descend into the tomb of Christ. This ceremony has its roots shrouded in obscurity. The Latin church has this ceremony, but it is a very modest one, consisting only of lighting a few candles in the church. I arose one morning very early and witnessed the celebrants come into the church and perform this rite. However, I knew that the Greek Orthodox celebration was the most exotic and exciting. I had seen pictures of hordes of people jamming the church, struggling to get the Holy Fire from the tomb of Christ. In these pictures I saw people hanging from the beams that supported the crumbling walls. They were clinging to the tops of the pillars. I knew that people had even been trampled to death as police struggled to control the passionate crowds, each one pushing and fighting to obtain some of the miraculous fire. One ancient historian writes that "on Easter Sunday an angel comes and lights the lamps that each may with it light up his own house." If at any time in history the sacred fire does not appear, and it is recorded that it happened at least once, it is looked upon as a judgment from God and tends to make the leaders temporarily reform their ways.

In 1981 I was conducting a tour near the Jaffa Gate, when I heard that on that very afternoon at one o'clock the ceremony of the Holy Fire would take place. I knew that this was the chance of a lifetime because I had never been in Jerusalem when this had taken place. I immediately turned my group over to my assistant and hurried down David Street to the Church of the Holy Sepulchre.

A group from NBC-TV was entering to photograph the event, and I saw also a youth group marching inside. I assumed that it would be normal for me to enter, and I slipped through the door. Immediately I knew that I had made a terrible mistake. I had just gotten through the door when I was swallowed up by a densely packed mass of black-gowned women and excited men. I could not move. I was caught in the viselike grip of a fanatical mob. It was impossible to retreat. I would have gladly forgotten about the Holy Fire, but it was too late. I could see the sunshine outside, but more people were pushing in, creating even more crowd density and confusion. I was nowhere near the tomb where the Holy Fire was to appear. I checked my watch and saw that it would be two hours before the supposedly miraculous event transpired. I knew I couldn't live through it for that long. I would never survive the suffocating heat, and the perspiration of hundreds of fighting, straining human bodies was sickening.

In that desperate moment I saw the figure that I now know was an angel. He was as tall as an NBA player, a blond, who looked like a German. He had been trapped like myself, with a couple of his friends. They stood between me and the door, and I could see he had resolved to escape. A voice within me said, "Grab hold of the blond man." I grasped his belt, hung on, and the battle began. The Germans were determined to break out, but the crowd was equally determined to prevent it. All reason had been abandoned in that awful crush of human bodies. The giant blond man with his friends towered above the black mass and formed a human wedge. The wall would not give way because of the angry and excited pressure behind it. It looked almost hopeless, but the blond and his group would not give up. Finally, a crack in the human wall appeared. The crowd finally broke, and we literally fell out through the breach into the sunlit courtyard.

When I had pulled myself to my feet the blond had vanished. Once again, as many years ago, I did not know, nor could I ever thank, my deliverer. I was bruised and numb from the ordeal. I stumbled back down the street leading to the Via Dolorosa, vowing I would never seek to see the Holy Fire again. I sat down in a coffee shop next to an Arab boy to recover my breath and my wits. With typical Arab grace he offered to share his bread and chicken with me, but I declined. I was not hungry and I was still in a state of shock.

As I relaxed there I thanked the Lord for that angel and for His marvelous deliverance. I somewhat recovered my composure. The words of David came to me:

"Our soul is escaped as a bird out of the snare of the fowlers" (Ps. 124:7).

After my narrow escape a huge crowd had gathered at the church. Even the rooftops were crowded with spectators. The bell tower of the church was crammed with eager faces peering down on the scene below. The air was charged with expectancy.

I was greeted warmly by the people waiting there. Many men and women were carrying candles. Evidently they were going to get enough of the Holy Fire to share with the folks at home. (I have heard that in earlier times people would have horses ready to dash to faraway places with the Holy Fire.) Russian ships were waiting to take the Holy Fire back to the homeland of the many Russian pilgrims.

As I sat that Easter Saturday waiting for the Holy Fire, I checked my watch. It was one o'clock in the afternoon, but still no sign. I wondered what was going on inside.

Suddenly an eerie phenomenon occurred. The air seemed to be filled with a supernatural force. The crowd swayed forward as if pushed by a mighty wind, though there was no sound at all. The thrilling feeling swept over me from head to foot. This momentary experience subsided, and the crowd lapsed back into waiting. In a few moments the same phenomenon was repeated.

Then it happened. Out of the church door burst a man bearing a flaming torch with the Holy Fire. He charged into the midst of the crowd with his smoking firebrand. The crowd went wild, crying out, "Christos anestis" ("Christ is risen") over and over. The people swarmed over the horse and its rider, reaching for the flame to light their candles. The air was full of fire and smoke. Soon another man dashed through the doors with a blazing torch. The crowd was almost crazed with a kind of holy joy. Faces glowed with happiness. The candles looked like a field of flaming red poppies waving in the wind. The crowd danced and whirled in exaltation.

Then the great bells of the church rang triumphantly. The sound swelled over the rooftops. The bells seemed to proclaim the Resurrection to the whole world. I took pictures as fast as I could to record the scene. Now I did not regret the danger and the physical suffering. I will always remember the mystical, moving force in the midst of that crowd, the eagerness for the Holy Fire, the joy of receiving and sharing.

I still wonder if at that moment I was seeing the church at her highest and best. I was reminded of Pentecost, with the mighty, rushing wind and the joy of the first disciples.

I returned to my group, inspired to tell them and the whole world, "Christ is risen."

TWELVE
ANGEL AT THE BERLIN WALL

Berlin — how can one describe the emotional impact of such a city? It assails you with the voice of fanatical chauvinism, brutality, conquest. It has the heartbeat of an "evil empire." Berlin was once one of the most cultivated, beautiful, imperial cities of the world. Its musicians, artists, and philosophers dominated the cultural atmosphere of the Continent and the world. Today its name is a synonym for barbarism. It speaks of a threat to the peace of humanity, of total war, of horrible genocide. It will take generations to expunge this guilt. Down its beautiful boulevards the Kaiser's minions once marched almost to the gates of Paris in 1914. Twenty-five years later the swaggering, goose-stepping Brownshirts of Der Fuehrer thundered again to achieve one of the great military conquests of history.

The first time I saw Berlin was in 1960. I came with a friend from an evangelistic tour of Northern Ireland. We swooped in over the rooftops into the Templehof Airport, which is, amazingly, located near the very heart of Berlin. Perhaps no other airport in the world offers such easy access. Berlin in 1960 was still very much an open city, except for the hostility that one could almost breathe in the highly charged atmosphere of the East Zone. But the city was wonderful. The sidewalks were crowded with people, and the cafes on the famous Kurfurstendamm were bursting with patrons. Stores overflowed with excellent consumer goods. At night the avenues of

West Berlin glowed with lights that reminded me of Chicago or Los Angeles. It still is a vibrant, fascinating city, but the next time I saw it, things had changed radically.

Berlin, 1966. I came with hundreds of delegates to the International Congress of Evangelism, one of the truly momentous religious gatherings of this century. It was conceived in the heart of Dr. Billy Graham and planned to be held at the heart of one of mankind's most troubled spots. From around the world 1,250 men and women came to fellowship, to study, to understand better how to proclaim the Good News. Doubtless the very fact that it was to be held in Berlin had a powerful attraction. I was an observer. Seats were extremely difficult to secure, and I felt very fortunate to be there. How can one condense into a few paragraphs the glory of those days? The sublime truth enunciated there by world-renowned speakers, the fellowship transcending all racial barriers defy description. Only a few miles from the German Democratic Republic — the nation building itself on antichrist philosophy — the Congress hall rang with the message of redemption. It penetrated into the very heart of the East Zone. It was an epochal confrontation between two world-conquering philosophies. Dr. Graham had just finished an extended evangelistic campaign in West Berlin, which had added to the frustration and opposition of the Communists. However, the tense atmosphere did not pervade the Congresshalle. The emphasis was, "The *kerygma* [the gospel message] must be proclaimed to the whole world." It was opened by a masterful address by the great theologian, Dr. Carl F. H. Henry.

On the Sunday of the Congress a massive demonstration was held. The entire body of the Congress marched down the Kurfurstendamm, their colorful national flags flying, to the remnant of the Kaiser Wilhelm Memorial Church. Here, in the shadow of this gaunt memorial to the destruction of Berlin, Dr. Graham challenged the whole world to acknowledge Christ as Savior, to avoid such future holocausts. What more fitting setting for such a reminder?

One priceless experience that came out of this conference was a visit to the Pergamum Museum in East Berlin. One morning at breakfast with Oral Roberts and Harold Kuhn (of Asbury Seminary), we were talking about the seven churches of Revelation. When I told Dr. Kuhn I had seen the sites of these churches in present-day Turkey, he asked if I knew of the Pergamum Museum in East Berlin. I almost jumped out of my chair in excitement. Without delay I took a subway to East Berlin. The great Pergamum Museum stood, miraculously undamaged, in the midst of bombed-out buildings. There stood the enormous temple which was taken out of Turkey by German archaeologists in the last century. What a miracle of preservation that was, and what a blessing it was to see this with my own eyes.

As uplifting as this trip to Berlin was, there was one shadow which fell over the Congress. It was the Wall, the Wall of Shame. It was first called this by Willy Brandt, mayor of West Berlin. I often walked down to see it. In 1960 I could go almost freely between the two zones. Now the obscene monument to tyranny and oppression slithered like a giant snake between the two sectors. On August 13, 1961, the inhabitants of East Berlin awoke to find that during the night they had been confined in a Communist prison.

After World War II, many people had "voted with their feet" to leave the Communist zone. The answer to this mass exodus to the West was the "petrified worm" obscenely crawling around Berlin, demolishing houses, stores, apartments, churches — in fact, everything in its path. Windows were boarded up, and every exit was closed. Everyone expected the Allied tanks to roll in, but as the occupying powers delayed action, the barbed wire went up. Every day the wall became more insurmountable. It soon became obvious that the wall was no Communist bluff.

One day during the Congress I climbed the platform where President John F. Kennedy had stood. The Communists had closed the view through the Brandenburg Gate with red curtains. When I stood there, however, I could see over the wall. How empty the streets, how lifeless the city. In spite of all the strong speeches and reassuring words, nothing was done except to protest, and the immoral wall rose stronger and stronger. The flowers I saw were all fresh on the graves of the escapees, the crosses adorned the pitiful mounds of those who failed in their dash to freedom. The wall was splashed with fierce graffiti condemning the merciless regime which mowed down the helpless with deadly volleys of machine gun fire. In the

death strip, murderous dogs barked constantly, relentless search-
lights probed the night, trip wires set off rockets, 150 watchtowers
lined the wall. It is now almost impossible to surmount the formi-
dable barriers and escape.

Yet the East Berliners proved how determined a desperate people
can become. Over the barbed wire with shredded flesh dripping
blood, they fell into the arms of the West Berliners. They hid in the
coal bins of locomotives, they crawled through sewers, they dropped
down into safety nets. The bewildered police leaped aside as huge
trucks blasted through the wall hurling blocks in all directions. One
escapee hid his fiancée in the trunk of his little car. Before attempting
to crash through, he measured the steel bar across the checkpoint.
He figured he had about an inch to spare. After deflating his tires
so as to make his car as low to the ground as possible, he roared
through, barely under the bar, to freedom, much to the astonish-
ment of the guards. One circus performer walked across the Spree
River on an electric cable, far out of reach of the deadly gunfire.
Hundreds of people escaped through tunnels painfully dug under
the wall. One of the most successful routes was through a crypt in
the churchyard of the Church of the Reconciliation, which was right
on the wall. Later, after many people had used this route, the tun-
nel was discovered and closed. But other ways have been tried, and
people continue to escape, their lives serving as a witness to the thirst
for freedom.

Perhaps the most famous of the checkpoints was in the American sector—Checkpoint Charlie. I had been through this before with
a busload of people from the Congress. Before we were readmitted
to West Berlin we were all unloaded from the bus, and hand trucks
with mirrors were run beneath the vehicle. This was because some
had escaped by hanging under the frame of the bus. It was all somewhat amusing—but not to those involved in the daily life and death
struggle with Communist oppression.

I had become quite familiar with this checkpoint because of my
frequent trips to the wall. The cruel wall fascinated me as I followed
its convolutions through the city. Perhaps because of this I had been
lulled into a false sense of security. On this particular day the Congress had adjourned. After a great farewell service and parade of

the flags the delegates left. I still had ample time before my plane left for Frankfurt, so I walked down again to Checkpoint Charlie. I climbed up into a viewpoint by the Wall and could see on a TV the activity on the other side. There was also a museum here which housed a fascinating collection of the devices used by the escapees to thwart the Wall. Among them was the famous little automobile that first drove through at high speed under the steel barrier. Some followed the example of this one, until the *Vopos* (police) lowered the barrier and put in more steel posts.

A large group of Americans were stationed about three hundred feet from the checkpoint. In recalling that near fatal day, I still find it difficult to explain why I permitted myself to become indifferent to the danger. There was no lack of warning signs. *Achtung!* ("Warning!") stood before the Brandenburg Gate. In several languages it read, "You are now leaving the American sector." I was having a good time shooting pictures of everything to show the folks back home. I was unaware that at the same time I was unconsciously advancing toward the barrier. A narrow white line marked the division between the East and West, but I did not see it. At that moment a rather poorly dressed lady came through toward me carrying a battered suitcase. She muttered something to me in German. I hesitated momentarily, but, not understanding German, I did not take it seriously.

I believe now that old lady was a guardian angel trying to obstruct my unconcerned way. How thankful I am that the Lord did not desert me, even after I still kept moving forward into danger!

On each side of the checkpoint there were bunkers where the *Vopos* kept guard every moment. In what has been called "The Battle of the Binoculars," Americans and Germans constantly checked each other, eyeball to eyeball. The East German officer was watching me intently through his binoculars — and I was looking intently at him! At that point I did a most dangerous thing—I raised my camera, and facing him straight ahead, I focused the guard right in the viewfinder of my camera and clicked the shutter. I still have that slide, revealing that officer watching me through his binoculars. I am confident now that I was being watched by many others. Very often at night I awake with perspiration breaking out all over me when I recall this confrontation. I can still see that hostile officer watching me; I can almost feel the bullets tearing through me. I fully believe that one more move forward, and I would have been dead. At that moment I know that a guardian angel spoke to me. The voice that I had heard so many times before said, "Turn around!" I did.

I looked over my shoulder and back at the entrance to the checkpoint, where the American soldiers were frantically waving at me and yelling for me to come back. Just then I looked down, and to my consternation I saw that the white line of the border was behind me. I was now in the East Zone, taking pictures of the *Vopos* and the installations in the death strip. All the weapons and the deadly arsenal of the strip were being trained on me. I was disregarding all the dangers and the traps that had been responsible for the death of seventy-two escapees. I am sure instant death faced me. I hurriedly turned and beat a hasty retreat to the shelter of the Americans. They were a very happy and relieved group of men when they welcomed me back to their end of the checkpoint.

I have been near death many times in my travels. Never would I be any nearer, I believe, than when I walked over that narrow, white line into the deadly, forbidden territory of East Germany. Others behind me saw my danger. The old lady with the battered suitcase saw it and tried to communicate with me.

Someone has said that David had two angels in Psalm 23 — Mercy and Goodness. I have had both of these qualities incarnated in a guardian angel. I owe my life to that angel's gentle ministrations.

THIRTEEN
ANGEL IN THE DESERT

We moved on toward Beersheba early in the afternoon. On that particular day of the tour, I was acting as the tour guide. Our driver was a Jew by the name of David. He was a tall, powerfully built, handsome man. He was quiet almost to the point of being taciturn. I was able to elicit information from him to the extent that he proudly admitted to being a veteran of all the wars of Israel.

The role of tour guide was a very unusual one for me. I have often been asked to serve in this role before, mostly because I have made so many trips to Bible lands, but I have never really been trained as a professional tour guide. I have met many wonderful guides on my trips to Israel. I think of Michael, a Jewish guide who was a treasury of inspiring knowledge. From the time he met us at the border until the time he left us he never stopped talking. He could answer all questions thrown at him.

Pity your poor guide. He has a busload of excited travelers who have come to Israel without much biblical background, and they can ask the most ignorant questions. The guide has to keep them together so that he can deliver his lecture, but many of the mavericks on the tour groups are drifting off, taking pictures, or looking everywhere else. At times half of his weary travelers are asleep in the back of the bus — not listening to what he has to say. He has to number every one in the bus before he starts — the safety and comfort of his flock are upon his shoulders. The halt and the lame, and sometimes even the blind, must be ushered safely on and off the bus. Anyone who becomes sick must be hospitalized, or drugs must be gotten immediately for that heart patient who has mislaid his nitroglycerine pills. Perhaps a group will go to the Jordan and some will run in excitedly with all their clothes on. Others defy all the rules and enter into forbidden places and end up in jail and have to be bailed out. Bones may be broken on a difficult step, ankles sprained, wheelchairs must be secured, the tour must go on. All this is the responsibility of the poor guide. How thankful we are to our guardian angels that they watch over us and hundreds of thousands who are safely and happily visiting the Holy Land every year.

We were on a narrow, hard-surfaced highway in the middle of the afternoon about halfway to Beersheba.

Ahead of us rolled a cement truck traveling at a rather slow rate of speed. Our bus was rolling up behind it quite swiftly, overtaking it just as it was beginning to climb a hill in front of us. There were no center lines and no warning signs against passing on a hill out there in the desert.

It was at this point that David, our driver, made a near fatal mistake. He elected to pass the cement truck on the hill. Any driver knows that passing a car on a hill is the cardinal sin of driving, an invitation to disaster. Countless people have lost their lives by taking that gamble. Yet who would conceive of there being any danger in the midst of the Negev desert? Apparently our driver did not think any existed. His vision was blocked only at that one point—everywhere else stretched out an endless sea of sand. The people in the group were nearly all asleep from the long journey that day—only I, our driver, and the guardian angel really witnessed the deadly drama just ahead.

The danger was approaching, however, like a rocket. A pickup truck driven by two Jews was in the other lane traveling toward us at high speed. It was hidden from the driver's view by the hill and the cement truck. It was at that point that David should have refrained from attempting to pass the truck ahead of us. Perhaps no soldier like him, who has been through several wars, ever treats danger seriously. David pulled around the end of the cement truck which put us exactly across into the opposite, oncoming lane. The driver of the cement truck was utterly unaware of the drama developing behind him, so he did not increase his speed, or alter it. I could see the mistake that our driver was making, but was speechless and powerless to prevent it. I never dreamed that death was just ahead in the Negev desert — just over the hill.

It is difficult to adequately describe this situation without making a diagram. As we pulled over into the other lane to complete our passing maneuver, the front end of our bus swung around the corner of the cement truck. At the same time the pickup came hurtling over the brow of the hill. Sitting on my side, I was placed directly in the path of the pickup, because of the angle of the approaching vehicle, and the direction of our bus. I was actually in more danger than the driver. A deep ditch on the right side of the road prevented the pickup from going over on that side. The Jews saw what was before them. Angels were hovering around us at that moment. I have not the slightest doubt of that fact. A crash seemed inevitable, and it would be fatal for me, for the driver, the Jews in the pickup, and for many of the passengers. In a split-second scenario I saw the whole, horrible catastrophe unfold. There was absolutely no way to escape it. The driver of the pickup chose absolutely the only course that could possibly have been taken — he made an utterly undreamed of decision. I saw the maneuver that he was about to make. Inwardly I cried, "No, he can't make it, there isn't room." But he did it — he shot through that narrow corridor like a jackrabbit. I braced myself for the shock that never came as the pickup flashed before my eyes, inches to spare to the other side of our lane and into the ditch, clearing both the back end of the rolling cement truck and the right hand corner of our bus.

For a few moments there was absolute silence, then the door of the bus opened and two shaken Jews came in. They were so shaken by their narrow escape, and ours, that they could not even talk. They only gestured with their hands and babbled out incoherent sounds in Hebrew. Our impassive driver did not even change expressions or speak a word. Perhaps he had been through more dangerous threats in his military life, but I doubt it. The passengers broke into a storm of applause. I knew, however, that they did not comprehend the nature of the near tragedy. I did, for I was sitting where I could have reached out and touched the pickup as it literally flew through. It was one of the most masterful pieces of driving I have ever seen. It was, indeed, accomplishing the impossible. I cannot doubt but that an angelic influence aided that pickup driver to measure that distance and go for it. I do not believe that it is humanly possible to make such quick decisions without divine help protecting us, and spreading angel wings over us.

We went on into Beersheba. I was shaken to the core by our narrow escape. How undeserved God's mercies are! His angels were that day shielding with their precious wings forty Holy Land passengers, and wafting a pickup truck through an impossible space.

FOURTEEN
ANGEL OVER THE CONGO

As I mentioned earlier, I am mistake-prone while traveling. Often-times the mistakes are of my own doing, but some have been due to others' bumbling. I recall one inexperienced travel agent who led me astray as I was preparing for a trip to South Africa. The agent told me to get my visa in New York at the South African consulate. At that time, as now, South Africa was extremely sensitive about world attitudes toward apartheid. I knew that, but I had no idea what problems would be involved in securing my visa. At the consulate I was interrogated suspiciously. I told the consulate personnel that I was going to South Africa to preach. This caused suspicion, as the National Council of Churches in the U.S. had voiced opposition to South Africa's racial policies. In other words, preachers were definitely suspect. The consulate people quizzed me further, then took my passport and told me to return the next day. My travel agent had failed to tell me that I should have told the consulate that I was simply traveling as a *tourist*. That minor oversight caused me to get a first-class runaround. And I never could make arrangements to visit South Africa. I had planned to preach the gospel there, but because of an inexperienced travel agent, I could not. However, God had opened other doors for me.

When I was finally able to retrieve my passport (this took a long time), I decided to go to the two tiny nations of Burundi and Rwanda in central Africa. The embassy offices of those two countries were gracious to me and granted me visas in only a few minutes. Soon I was off to central Africa by way of Cairo.

When I arrived, the airport at Bukavu (in Zaire, formerly the Belgian Congo) was manned by heavily armed black guards carrying machine guns. They eyed me menacingly as I stepped off the plane. Shortly before I arrived, a holocaust had taken the lives of many people. The world then was aware of the horrors of the Vietnam War but almost totally unaware of the slaughter in these tiny countries, a slaughter which claimed more lives than what was occurring in Vietnam.

In spite of the political climate, my ministry in Burundi and Rwanda was fulfilling in many respects. During my brief stay I had opportunities to speak in the schools, visit the hospitals, and fellowship with the devoted missionaries and Christian natives. I had the experience of being a firsthand observer of the many changes taking place in Africa. Yet I was not able to minister to the degree I wished. And in the midst of my visit I received a telegram from South Africa, granting permission for my visa. I was pleased at this, though I then became aware that my time in central Africa was limited.

My only opportunity to preach to a large congregation came on my last Sunday in Burundi. The church there was one of the largest in my denomination. It was filled with a huge congregation of men sitting on benches and women reclining on the dirt floor. As I tried to bring God's message that morning, I experienced the frustration of having a poor interpreter. He spoke in a dull, metallic tone, apparently trying to convey the words correctly without getting personally involved. While some interpreters seem almost inspired in their ability to communicate the preacher's words and feelings, this one was definitely not inspired. As a result, the sermon never did "catch fire."

An added frustration was the women, who were constantly conversing in a low tone. I could not rise above this subdued murmur. In desperation, I picked up the heavy stick the song leader had used to pound the drum while leading the singing. I gave a few sharp blows on the drum, and this helped momentarily, but soon the women resumed their conversation. When I gave the invitation at the sermon's end, only five people came forward. I was extremely frustrated, and I spent the remaining hours that Sunday praying and trying to find an answer for my apparent failure. The missionaries thought the service was excellent, but I felt it was drab and barren. So it was in a mood of frustration that I left for my return to the U.S.

Getting out of Burundi was complicated. The only plane for Cairo left but once a week, from Bujumbura. A large crowd was waiting at the airport to get passage. I was taken to the airport by the missionary in charge, and he ushered me into the rather primitive airport and helped me to arrange my ticket and check my baggage. He was not allowed beyond that point, and he was the only English-speaking person there, except a Belgian officer. The missionary could help no more. Because of the large crowd and because I had a long wait, I had resolved to be the very first one on the plane. I did not even sit down, but posted myself right by the door leading out to the plane so as to be sure of a good seat. I saw my baggage going by on the rollers, and was congratulating myself that everything was in order. One view of the plane convinced me that my plans were strategic, as it was a second-class machine.

After a long wait, the call to board came over the sound system. I started to move confidently toward the plane. The attendant at the door, who did not speak a word of English, motioned for my boarding pass. To my utter horror, I realized that I had failed to get it before leaving the ticketing area. The missionary had failed to notice this, and the person in charge had not given me one automatically. The lady at the door refused to let me through in spite of all my anguished pleadings. In agony I watched as all the people in the departure lounge pushed by me onto the plane, and I was left standing there alone with no boarding pass, without my missionary friend, and with no one who could understand English. I looked around frantically for someone to help me, but no one appeared. I do not remember to this day how I finally secured my boarding pass — I only know that an angel touched someone and it came. As I rushed out to the plane again, a Belgian officer halted me and pointed to a suitcase that was standing all by itself some distance away on the platform. I had assumed, naturally, that it had gone on the plane. The official said: "Is that your case out there?" I thought I would faint.

"Yes, it is," I replied. Here was another frustrating problem. My case, for some unknown reason, had been set off to one side. I will never know why—perhaps custom regulations had not been met somehow, or it may have looked suspicious for an unknown reason. Or perhaps God was testing my faith.

I know that an angel intervened. The Belgian hesitated, and waved me on with my suitcase. As I rushed to the plane, which was about to take off, I saw out of the corner of my eye my suitcase actually going on—the very last piece of baggage on the plane. I silently thanked the Lord and took courage.

As I climbed aboard the aircraft, it looked as if it had been resurrected from some World War II junk heap. I reflected, in horror, "We have to fly this all the way to Cairo—three thousand miles." It was unusually constructed, in that there were four compartments—the captain's and crew's compartment, the main compartment or economy, a first-class compartment, and a mail compartment, paneled with unpainted plywood between the captain's and the central compartment.

As I entered, the stewardess led me up to the front into this special mail compartment. This was completely filled, some of the passengers being Belgian priests returning home. It was extremely hot in these closed quarters. About the time that we took off the priests got out big cigars and began to smoke. Soon the compartment was saturated with dense tobacco smoke. I contemplated with horror the thought that we would be flying all night in this stuffy, smoke-laden atmosphere, in a plane with primitive, uncomfortable seats. It seemed a fitting finale to a trouble-filled, frustrating trip to the mission fields.

We stopped at a place called Marysville to refuel before we went further north. In fact we had to reverse our flight and go south to secure fuel, before heading out over the jungles for our long journey to Cairo. As we stopped to refuel I rushed off the plane to see for sure if by now my suitcase was aboard. I was sure of nothing. I asked the attendants if they would open the baggage compartment and check for my suitcase. They complied with this unusual request

with great courtesy. To my great relief it was there, on the very outside near the door.

The Congo was in turmoil at this time. The Belgians had left the
country that they had administered since World War I with their
customary efficiency and ruthlessness. The struggle to fill the vacuum
which followed resulted in a horrible bloodbath. (The Simbas, or
"Lions," had taken over the Congo in a bloody coup that cost the
lives of many missionaries, including the famous Dr. Carlson. His
death and that of others is related in the well-known book, *Out of
the Mouth of the Lion.*) It was not comforting to me to think of what
might be the fate of a white man, especially a Christian, in those
vast jungles below as we flew over them. To add to the discomfort,
a thunderstorm arose, and soon we were tossing around like a chip
on a wave, as we cruised through the air currents. These planes were
not the powerful jets of today which can soar above such storms and
cruise so smoothly that they would not spill a glass of water. We were
struggling against adverse weather conditions that made me feel
at times that all of our movement was vertical and not horizontal.
The long night that I was facing, confined in this narrow compartment, squeezed into these uncomfortable seats, stifled with tobacco
smoke, unable to sleep with hour after hour of misery before we
got to Cairo, if we ever did in such weather, terrified me.

Then an angel intervened. There are some things in our lives
which cannot be explained on a rational basis. Those who cherish
a living faith in Christ cannot reject these things as simply coinci-
dence or accident. The airliner captain stopped by my seat and said,
"We are going to move you!" I was bewildered. Why would they move
me? The whole cabin was full of hot, miserable people, tossing up
and down in the miserable aircraft. Where would they move me?

He said, "We are going to take you back to the first-class compartment!" I had never ridden in one of them. Economy was the
best I could ever afford.

I had looked with envy many times at the wide, comfortable seats
in the first-class section, and viewed the stewardesses serving special meals to the passengers long before we received ours. As the
curtain was pulled to give them privacy, I imagined all sorts of
privileges that they enjoyed, which were not for the economy

passengers. In fact, I was quite surprised that they had a first-class compartment in that miserable aircraft.

So I was singled out of the group in that inferno of smoke in the compartment and led by the stewardess back to the rear of the plane. The first-class compartment was empty, except for one lady passenger. It was air-conditioned. The stewardess deposited me into the softest, most comfortable seat that I think I ever occupied in my life, as the cooling stream of air floated all over my perspiring, weary body. It seemed that I was floating on the clouds of heaven — I had been transported in a moment to the unbelievable ethereal realms of bliss. How could I have ever rated this?

The enjoyment of that experience is beyond description. After having been there a few moments I forgot all about the thunder that was rolling all around, the pitching of the airplane as we bored through the masses of clouds around us, the frightening horror in the jungle below — it was sheer bliss.

Sabena Airlines was famous for its cuisine. I found that the glowing reports were justified. Before the food was served, I was brought a pair of bedroom slippers in which to rest my aching feet on the long flight to Cairo. Then the attendants gave me a bottle of perfume to dispel the pungent smoke from the other compartment. I was even given a beautiful tie pin with the Sabena insignia. It was a lovely reminder of a great experience.

The Belgian coffee was delightful, served not in plastic cups but in fine dinnerware. Then the main meal came, with everything to titillate the appetite of a jaded traveler like myself. The white-clad chef came in, pushing a tea cart carrying a huge roast. I saw that he was about to slice off a huge piece that was somewhat on the rare side. I mentioned that I preferred mine well done, and he replied, "No problem, monsieur." He wheeled the cart around, took it back to the galley, then brought it back in a few minutes, done to perfection. The large slices were delicious.

This was service deluxe to a passenger who for the last month had been plagued by constant frustrations. I was the pampered guest of an airline, which, unknowingly, had been the servant of an angel. I could not understand, but I reveled in the mystery. After a marvelous dessert, served in the same exquisite style, I sank into the soft seat propped up by spotless pillows, cooled by streams of air, and spent one of the most restful nights of my life in an airplane. The pitching of the plane in the turbulent air currents, the twisting in a narrow seat to get a few minutes of tortured sleep had vanished.

Why was I chosen out of all that group in the unpainted plywood compartment unless it were from an angel? It seemed those Belgian priests would have a priority over me. I was not wearing any kind of ecclesiastical insignia. It is like many of the gifts of God. We cannot explain them, we just believe and rejoice in them.

I could not help but feel sorry for my fellow passengers up ahead in those narrow seats, trying to be comfortable with a little plastic box, covered with cellophane on their laps, bent over between the rows crowded together so as to get every one they could on the only plane going out of Burundi. Here I lolled on these wide seats, all by myself, which ordinarily seated at least three people, with air-conditioning blowing all around.

When I awoke, the sun was blazing through the window of the airliner. We were approaching Cairo. I had been spared a long night of misery. Below me were the imperishable pyramids of Khufu, Khafra, and Menkura and the mighty brooding Sphinx — tiny stone monuments in a vast ocean of golden sand. As we dropped into the airport the Arab thanksgiving welled from my heart: *Shukran le Rabbah* —Thank the Lord!

FIFTEEN
ANGEL IN ATHENS

Athens — who can pronounce the name without wonder and reverence? There, 2,500 years ago, flowered such genius as has never been surpassed, or perhaps never even equalled. Succeeding ages have imitated its architecture, admired its philosophy, been enamored by its loveliness, and tried to copy its democracy. The great thinkers whom Athens produced in its golden age challenge our most advanced concepts with their encyclopedic minds. At the height of its greatness in the fifth century B.C., heroic citizens defeated the massed, barbaric Persian hordes at Marathon and Plataea. As we go to Corinth today along the Bay of Salamis, we see where Xerxes sat in his golden chair upon the mountain above the great naval battle, and watched with horror as the courage of the numerically inferior Greeks and the cunning of the great Themistocles sent his great fleet to the bottom of the sea. Greece that day saved Western civilization.

A flood of emotion swept over me as I recalled the history of that marvelous building uplifted on the sacred hill against the blue dome of heaven. It was, and still is, the most beautiful and perfect structure ever constructed by man. Upon that tiny hilltop only 512 feet high was nursed more genius than half the empires of the world. I have seen many enormous temple complexes, but none can compare with that exquisite jewel, the Parthenon. The proportions of the Parthenon have inspired the architects of all ages — first the Roman, then the buildings of the Renaissance period, then those of our own time.

Socrates claimed that he had a guardian angel, a divine voice which aided him in his decisions. This, as we understand it, is the chief ministry of guardian angels. If Socrates, the noblest of pagan philosophers, without any biblical assistance, could be convinced of this ministry of angels, why cannot I or any Christian claim for himself the same glorious companion?

I have never been far from angelic protection. I certainly needed it, for what seemed to me to be a heaven in Athens was metamorphosed into a dreadful nightmare of danger. My sister, who is a registered nurse and who has accompanied me on many trips to Bible lands, had advised me to take some preventive medicine against digestive upsets. I did not take her seriously, but when she met me in Chicago she insisted, and loaded me down with paregoric and other pills, which I reluctantly accepted. Hardly had we left the U.S. when trouble struck. One of our group, a well-known conservative seminary teacher, fell victim to a stomach disorder. When it was learned that I was equipped with medicine, my supply quickly began to dwindle.

After seeing the majestic ruins of Athens we were transported to a restaurant en route to Corinth. Everything seemed normal as far as cleanliness was concerned, and being hungry with our exertions in travel we all partook of it unsuspectingly. Late in the afternoon of that gorgeous day I began to feel a slight discomfort as I walked the streets of downtown Athens. I thought that it was only from some chocolate candy I had purchased and that it would soon vanish, but the pain continued to increase in intensity.

All efforts to obtain relief failed. (I was not the only one in the group who had a problem, but the others were finding remedies — some of which they had borrowed from me.) I seemed to be becoming paralyzed as far as my digestive system was concerned. I was ordinarily a very healthy person, yet I was completely immobilized physically. I concluded that I had been poisoned. I became tremendously weak from constantly trying to activate my digestive tract. I was scheduled to preach in the Evangelical Mission in Athens that night, and knew it would have to be cancelled, a painful decision to make. The day wore on, with still all my attempts to obtain relief totally ineffectual.

I knew I had been poisoned. All of the medications which my sister had given me were gone. To increase my agony, I knew that the rest of my group were out seeing the glorious sights of Athens and I was here alone.

The awful thought crossed my mind: "I am dying. Here I am ten thousand miles away from home. I am alone, away from the tour group, and I am going to die in Athens." I was convinced that this would be the outcome of this dreadful poison that had gripped me with its deadly power.

Many times an angel has spoken to me in the years of my pilgrimage. Let others call it what they will, I lift my heart in gratitude to that unseen mentor of my life who has always been with me in these life-threatening experiences.

A voice said, "Pull your fingers together to a point, and shove them down your throat as far as you can." In desperation I obeyed and thrust my fingers so far down my esophagus that I thought they would touch my stomach. Then, the ugly mass came up. The poisonous lump was as black as coal. It was nothing like one would experience in a simple stomach upset. What relief! I fell onto the floor—weak, but alive! I crawled to my bed, delivered from a mass of deadly poison that I was sure was going to kill me. In a few days my weight had dropped from 206 to 180. My friends scarcely recognized me when I finally arrived at home.

As a firm believer in Romans 8:28 ("All things work together for good to them that love God") I can now see how that dreadful experience has worked for me. I am confident that an immunity has been granted to me that has been of inestimable value, so that in traveling for thirty years in over sixty countries under every conceivable circumstance, my stomach has never been more than mildly upset a couple of times. This has been especially true on the many mission fields where the natives exhaust their meager funds to prepare a magnificent meal to show their hospitality and love. To refuse them is to risk mortally offending them, yet you know that the "but" lurks in every dish. After having done my very best at times to escape partaking of such hospitality, I have been forced to yield and eat with the natives. Yet I have never become ill, while at the same time others with me have become very ill. My Athenian experience has never been repeated.

SIXTEEN
ANGEL AT TORREMOLINOS

One of the most outstanding spiritual events of this century was the International Congress of Itinerant Evangelists in Amsterdam, the Netherlands, in July 1983. It was the Congress of the forgotten man, the evangelist. At the invitation of Dr. Billy Graham, over four thousand evangelists gathered in the RAI, one of the largest convention complexes in Europe, to fellowship, pray, listen, and learn how to better evangelize their world. One thousand observers, visitors, press people, and others swelled the attendance to five thousand. Some of the big names were there, to be true, but it was most noticeable that the Third World had invaded Amsterdam and demonstrated that they were a vital force for evangelism in our day.

Europe seemed to me to be a continent of ice, spiritually speaking. So to me the most impressive part of the Congress was the massive effort to take the gospel into Amsterdam itself and the surrounding areas. Delicious packaged lunches were prepared for everyone, and, armed with Billy Graham's booklet *Steps to Peace with God,* three thousand evangelists went rolling out into the Netherlands. While on the buses, we sang "Freely ye have received, freely give," a line from "Freely, Freely," the theme song of the conference.

Dr. Graham had warned us to expect some unusual sights on the Dutch beaches, and his words were well taken. The beaches were a mass of human flesh, and one could see evangelists witnessing to seminude sunbathers. I recall one African evangelist witnessing to a topless woman. When he returned to his white American friends, they asked him why he didn't feel uncomfortable witnessing under such circumstances. He smiled and replied, "Where I work, none of the women cover their breasts. To me it would have seemed strange if she had been wearing the top half of her bathing suit!" Dr. Graham himself went about incognito, wearing a T-shirt, slacks, hat, and sunglasses. He remarked on the effectiveness of the Africans in witnessing to the Europeans, an ironic situation when one considers that it was the Europeans who had first brought the gospel to the peoples of central and southern Africa. I myself had difficulty in outreach, but I prayed constantly over this very difficult evangelistic effort. In the evening service, about five hundred decisions for Christ were reported. Great excitement was generated as we again sang, "Freely ye have received."

A friend of mine who was attending the Congress was a worker with Spanish-speaking people in the U.S. He wanted to go to Spain to perfect his conversational technique. He and his wife invited me to go with them, an invitation which I accepted with alacrity. My veins felt the faster coursing of my blood at the very possibility of visiting this entrancing country. Having read the *Tales of the Alhambra* when I was a child, I was enthralled by the magic of Granada. In the early 1970s I had made a stop for a brief look at Madrid and Avila, but this was an unprecedented opportunity to see the land of my dreams—Andalusia, in southern Spain.

Our rented car was very small and uncomfortable, but one does not permit such inconveniences to deter him when he is about to see the fulfillment of the dream of a lifetime. Sitting crossways on the car's backseat while my friend and his wife occupied the front, I had an uninterrupted view of Europe as it unrolled before us.

We were soon in Castile and Leon, the heart of ancient Spain where the purest Spanish is spoken—Castilian. The country appeared to be desperately poor, and the drive was void of places of scenic interest until we came to Burgos, the capital of old Castile. Here was to open to me a new chapter in my travels, the cathedrals of Spain. No matter how poor the province, how wretched the peasantry, the cathedral rises and dominates with splendor.

I have seen countless cathedrals in Europe, the British Isles, and America in my travels. In a manner of speaking, if you have seen one you have seen them all. Cathedral building in the Middle Ages was quite standardized. The cathedrals of Europe are imposing in size and grandeur, but they generally followed the same design. I was not prepared for the cathedrals of Spain. They were like no cathedrals I had ever seen. Burgos Cathedral was only the first that opened my eyes to a new world of beauty. It staggered me from the first moment I saw the unique highly ornamented entrance to the interior that seemed to explode with a variety of colors and myriads of figures adorning every part. The richness of detail dazzled me. It was almost ethereal. Painting of an earlier day did etherealize the Burgos Cathedral. Little did I realize that this was only the introduction to some of the grandest monuments of man's genius.

Then after Burgos there was Segovia. The traveler in Spain halts in awe when suddenly he comes upon the splendor of old Segovia. The city is a fascinating amalgam of Roman and Moorish and Christian cultures. The Alcazar, a castle that looks as if it were perched in the sky, seems like the stuff of dreams. The most stupendous structure is the two-thousand-year-old Roman aqueduct which marches across the avenue into the city. It is the most perfect structure of its kind in the world. It looks as if it were good for another two thousand years. Until recently it furnished water for the city. The blocks themselves were so artfully put together that they needed no mortar. For a quarter of a mile it runs athwart the city almost untouched by the relentless encroachment of time. Incredibly it has survived the forces that have doomed the greater part of the civilizations of antiquity. I had seen it before with absolute incredulity when its two layers of arches, one upon another framed the blue sky, with pastel-soft patina colors glowing.

In Madrid we secured a humble pension right off the Gran Via and right across from McDonald's restaurant! The famous home of the golden arches must at one time have been a bank building, for the floors were of marble, the balconies were supported by pillars of granite. Such a McDonald's could not be found anywhere else in the world.

The time had come for me to say farewell to my friends and to launch out on my own for the long anticipated trip to Andalusia in southern Spain. How were they to know that they would be robbed of their travel documents at that same McDonald's and be forced to stay another hectic, frustrating, and expensive week in Madrid? How was I to foresee that I would experience a close brush with the Black Angel of Death? Fortunately, a wise Providence conceals these calamities from us.

I found that I could take a five-day, all-expense-paid trip by bus for only eighty-five dollars. I was on a bus with an almost 100 percent Spanish-speaking group, and I felt very isolated. After I had traveled on this bus for a couple of days I found that there were some who did speak English, more or less.

We were en route to Torremolinos, eight miles southwest of Malaga. In Torremolinos eighty-two high-rise hostelries all but blot out sea and earth and sky. So many restaurants line the Call Cauce — the Spaniards call it "the Street of Hunger." As usual, I was very much on my own because of the nature of the group in the bus. After five days I still had very little communication with them except with a Cuban couple from New Jersey. Hence, I spent much of my time that day after arriving from Granada walking up and down the sidewalk which ran for miles down the beach crowded with bathers. Next to the sidewalk was a highway, running, according to my map, all the way to Gibraltar, which was about one hundred miles to the southwest. While this was not a superhighway, it was the only road and it was exceedingly dangerous, as I later learned.

After relaxing along the beautiful beach for the afternoon, I retired to a nice apartment right across the street, from which I had a marvelous view of the ocean in both directions. A lovely little balcony gave me a rather special observation post.

Morning dawned clear and beautiful. In Spain no one moves before eleven in the morning. No breakfast was in sight, so I decided once more to take the stroll down the sidewalk and view the beautiful Mediterranean sunrise, which was just beginning to illuminate the east with glory. I walked slowly back to the motel to cross over and prepare to leave.

That morning on the Costa del Sol as I walked toward the motel, two specks were bearing down on me out of the distance — two cars traveling at a high speed. The highway was empty, except for these two cars in the early morning hours. I made the mistake of not going clear to the crosswalk, for there was one marked, but it was beyond my motel. I am not sure now that it would have prevented what was happening anyway. In addition to making the mistake of not using the crosswalk, I underestimated the speed of the approaching vehicles. As I started across the street I assumed that they would slow down when they saw me crossing. The callousness of some European drivers is almost inhuman. They did not slow down — they even seemed to increase their velocity. In violation of all rules of traffic they were occupying both lanes. One was somewhat behind the other. I found myself unable to retreat — I had gone too far. I have dodged cars by the thousands in over sixty countries of the world, but this was unlike any car-dodging situation I had ever faced. Imagine the brutish callousness of drivers, observing a pedestrian in such a predicament and yet unwilling to reduce their speed.

The two specks became thunderbolts hurled at me. I was exactly in front of car No. 1. By acting quickly I stepped clear of him and he roared on. The two had been almost side by side — with the yellow line between them. No. 2 car bore down on me. I was almost crushed between them. I knew I could not evade the second one.

Then the impossible happened again. The voice of an angel said, "Jump." It was the same voice that spoke so many years ago when I was attacked by a mad bull — that so many times since has energized me in a supernatural way. "Jump," it said. That was the last thing in the world that I could have done in my own strength. To have taken one step further would have doomed me to be crushed under car No. 2. There was no time to think this over. I obeyed that voice as before, and something seemed to literally lift me in the air. I jumped higher than I ever had in my life and soared right over the front of the car and landed prostrate on the grass on the other side. Car No. 2 never slowed down, and the driver never even looked to see what happened. I doubt if he would have stopped had he hit me. It would have been a magnificent leap in any competition because it was propelled by angelic, supernatural force. I lay there shaking, bathed in perspiration from every pore, but happy to be alive. I knew that I had escaped death in the closest encounter in a lifetime of peril. I heard the cars roar away, the drivers utterly insensitive and oblivious to the tragedy that an angel had averted.

The burden of proof is on the skeptic. What was that unseen force that enabled me — a man seventy-six years old — to accomplish such a tremendous leap? No human solution is adequate. An angel had placed his wings under me again that morning and lifted me right over to safety. I was the most shaken person in Spain that day. My brush with the Angel of Death had been averted by the ever faithful Angel of Life, but it had left me so weak I could scarcely stand. I went to my room with no appetite for food or conversation. I was almost paralyzed and speechless. All the way to Madrid the awful scene was reenacted again and again in my mind, as well as numberless times since.

I was horrified — but overwhelmingly grateful. God had sent his angel to deliver me again. He performed the impossible. He gave me a few more years to glorify his name and to carry on my life's work.

SEVENTEEN
ANGEL AT THE GARDEN TOMB

I first came to the Holy Land to fulfill the wonder of a lifelong dream. When I left my wife and girls, I was laden with some apprehension. I had never flown before. I carried a load of almost unbearable grief. The flowers on the grave of my son, Gerald, had withered since that beautiful Good Friday when we said one last farewell as his casket lay on the straps, covered with the school colors from which he had expected to graduate in six weeks. But time, with its healing balm, had not yet soothed the pain.

Our only son, a young man of twenty-one, had been killed about six months before. It was springtime in Seattle then, and how lovely were the sights and sounds of that Easter weekend. Our anticipations were running high, for our son had a wonderful charisma. Young and old adored him. Just a friendly touch from him, and the bond of fellowship was sealed. He was engaged to a beautiful girl who that year was the Queen of the May, and he led her to the throne in the midst of the campus. Gerald was preparing for the mission field, and we were looking forward to his attending seminary in the fall.

On that night of April 16, 1954, on a Good Friday weekend, as I was in the district parsonage idly chatting with my wife and girls, the phone rang. Thinking that it was only another of the many calls that I, as superintendent, would receive, I went to the phone only to be informed by the operator that Gerald had been seriously injured. We never dreamed of the nature of the injury from the telephone call. We hastened to the car, sped across town to the hospital, only on arriving to hear the awful words: "He's gone." His head had been crushed by a piece of machinery while he was working with some boys from the college on a church. His last words were, "Oh, Jesus, help me." I rushed with my family to his side, and kissed his still warm face, for he had died on the operating table. I had fully expected that when my mantle would slip from my failing shoulders that he would pick it up and minister even much more effectively. I had tasted of Good Friday but not yet of Easter Sunday. The cup that I drank that dark night was so bitter. The unanswered questions were so difficult to resolve.

On Christmas Eve in the Holy Land our group had gone to Bethlehem. We had worshiped with an interdenominational group sponsored by the YMCA at the Shepherds' Cave near Bethlehem. We ate barbecued mutton sandwiches that had no butter, but plenty of ashes. I could not eat mine, but a bright-eyed little Arab boy from the refugee camp nearby lurked in the bushes, hungrily watching us eat. I handed my unfinished sandwich to him, and he grabbed it like a hungry little wolf and darted back into the shadows. Our group scattered. Some went to the Church of the Nativity for the Latin service, but I returned to the Ambassador Hotel. The hotel had been used for a military post in the 1948 war. The work of rebuilding and finishing had not yet been completed, and it was cold and uninviting. I felt dreadfully isolated. The grief seemed unbearable. I had never before been separated from my family at Christmas. A wave of sorrow swept me upon the cliffs of something like despair.

Christmas Day dawned gloriously under cloudless skies. The ideal time to visit the Garden tomb is in the early morning before the crowds gather. I went there hunting for solace for my pain and loneliness. Not a soul was near to mar that sacred hour, as I met with my Savior in the Garden. I stood by the open door of the tomb and looked within. Someone seemed to stand beside me in the likeness of an angel, and he said to me, "Your son is not here. He is risen." All my sorrow vanished. The tears flowed, but now they were tears of joy. I left the Garden triumphantly, to continue my journey and to experience the wonders of which I had dreamed so long.

EIGHTEEN
ANGEL ON THE
MOUNT OF OLIVES

1982. Jerusalem at Easter—what better place to be in the world? Our group had gone to the six o'clock morning service. Sunday had dawned with the empyrean blue skies of Jerusalem arching over us with a dome of glory. It was business as usual with the Arabs, but enormous numbers of Christian pilgrims were gathering at the tomb and filing through the narrow street between high walls leading to the Garden. The golden walls of Jerusalem were still sleeping, untouched by the dawn. The fragrance of countless flowers was in the air, and the birds were adding their symphony of praise. *Anastasis*—resurrection—was in our hearts!

Yet in the midst of this climactic act of pilgrimage and celebration of our faith, who was to know that a deadly time bomb was ticking away, soon to explode with such power as to shake Jerusalem to the very foundations, as it had so often been in history!

After breakfast we went as a tour group to visit the sites of the city that had been scheduled for the day. We entered through the ancient Dung Gate and were checked through in a routine examination by the soldiers at the entrance. Many Jews were at the Western Wall, or, as it was once called, the Wailing Wall.

We had been detained by the guide from entering into the area of the Western Wall because of the numerous Jews that were already there. Suddenly, as we were waiting, we heard two, sharp, ringing rifle shots. Two young soldiers who had been guarding the entrance to the plaza left and ran at top speed to the gate. The reaction around us was varied. One Jew said, "Oh, it's only a practice exercise." Another beside me growled, "Blow it down, so that we can build the temple." This is a hope that burns in the hearts of many Orthodox Jews. They pray that some disaster like a stroke of lightning or an earthquake will demolish Haram, or Dome of the Rock, so that the temple can be rebuilt in its place.

The Arabs are well aware that this feeling exists, not only among Jews, but among many fundamentalist Christians. The Israelis are keenly aware of this dangerously explosive situation. The last thing they want is to see damage of any sort happen to the mosques. If for no other reason, it undermines their claim that they can guard the sacred sites more successfully than any other claimant. They boast that under their administration religious freedom in the Holy City is enjoyed as it never has been in all of the centuries. The Muslim hours of worship are very strictly guarded. No non-Muslims are allowed in the square at those times. Israel has an admirable track record in this respect, and their claims to success are justified.

The firing now became heavier. It sounded like automatic rifles or even machine guns. It was clear this was no practice exercise but the real thing.

The Israeli soldiers began to pour in with jeeps and ambulances. It appeared that they *had* practiced for just such a crisis as this. The soldiers were now herding the reluctant, fur-hatted, Orthodox Jews away from the wall. Soon heavier firing began to mingle with the light, sharp shots. Sharpshooters appeared upon the walls. I looked to the guide for an explanation, but he would not answer. The fear was showing from his eyes. His face seemed pale under his dark, brown skin. He was trying to move us up Mount Zion, away from the danger.

He had trouble getting us to move, as we stood fascinated. I stood near to a Jew in his prayer cap and shawl, praying mightily as the shots were being fired. He was swaying up and down — totally oblivious to everything around him. Had I understood, I might have heard him praying for destruction of the mosque. Now the voice from the minaret, one of the mosque's tall towers, began to sound. But this was not a call to prayer. It had an ominous, frightening note. Although I could not understand, I learned later that it was calling Arabs everywhere to the battle that was building up in the square. The sound was booming out everywhere, resounding off the Mount of Olives, bouncing off the city walls, "Come to the square, the Jews are trying to take over the mosque." They were responding in great numbers, coming from everywhere, pouring through the city gates to take part in what they feared was a struggle for the mosque. The Arabs are not allowed guns, but they possess knives, clubs, staves, and that lethal weapon, the rock. Inside the square was a huge mob of raving, screaming men, throwing rocks and working themselves into a terrible frenzy.

An antiterrorist squad of Israelis now marched up the steps to the temple area, where they were confronted and stoned by Muslim youth.

The cause of all this was an apparently demented Jewish soldier from Baltimore, Maryland, Allan Harry Goodman. Shortly after nine in the morning that Easter Sunday, the burly and bearded Goodman entered the Temple Mount through the Ghawanima, the northernmost gate in the western side of the Mount. Dressed in army uniform and carrying an American-made M-16 rifle, which is widely used in the Israeli Defense Forces (IDF), Goodman shot and wounded a guard who tried to stop him at the gate. Goodman then ran toward the magnificent golden-domed Muslim shrine, firing at every Arab he saw. A fifty-five-year-old guard at the Dome of the Rock was shot dead at the entrance to the shrine. Goodman climbed upon the great Foundation Stone, where Abraham is said to have planned to sacrifice his son, Isaac, and from which the Muslims believe that Muhammad ascended to heaven on his horse Barak. Goodman fired out through the main door of the Dome of the Rock until two magazines were empty. Fully loaded, each magazine could hold thirty bullets. With drawn guns, several officers slipped into the shrine through another door, taking shelter behind the columns. They grabbed Goodman, who surrendered quietly. When asked why he had done it, he said, "They kill Jews every day. I had to do it."

We could not see this taking place, of course. We viewed it on TV later. Now the problem was getting Goodman out through the roaring Arab mob. Pushing Goodman ahead of them, the officers opened a door on the south side of the shrine, and ran for the Moghrabi Gate opposite us. We did not see this part of the episode. By that time our guide had hurried us out of there.

The crowd broke after the Israeli soldiers, according to an Israeli eyewitness. It seemed that the police and their prisoner would be engulfed by the mob, which was shouting "Allah uh-Akbar" ("God is great"). The soldiers managed to reach the area of the gate where waiting police with drawn guns formed a cordon. Goodman was hustled down the ramp to the Western Wall plaza and taken to police headquarters for questioning. Police meanwhile cut the wires to al-Aqsa Mosque minaret's public address system to prevent any more appeals to come to the Temple Mount. For two hours Arab youths with staves and knives and rocks demonstrated on the Temple Mount. As I viewed the TV reports of the young Arabs throwing rocks, I was unaware that I was soon to learn how lethal a hard-thrown rock can be. During this time the Israeli soldiers had continued to pour into the area surrounding the wall until it resembled an army encampment.

In the meantime the Arab Council had met and shut down the city. It had also ordered all airports in the Arab world to suspend operations. It was eerily quiet in the Old City. As we slowly left the area, lingering to get one last glimpse of the dangerous melee, we found that every shop by now in the Old City was buttoned down. It was a queer sensation to feel the utter silence that had settled down — somehow we felt as we moved along that hundreds of eyes were looking at us as we silently wended our way toward the Damascus Gate.

When we arrived there, another serious crisis confronted us. The great gate was blocked by a mob of shoving, shouting Arabs, commanded by the leader of the Arabs on the West Bank. They were demanding to get into the city and to join the fray on the Temple Mount. They had been blocked, however, by two young Israeli soldiers, with guns laterally held against the bodies pressing upon them. The excited crowd was shoving hard to enter. I was aware that if the soldiers would be suddenly forced to give way, they might be provoked into shooting, and terrible would be the consequences for all of us.

While the crowd was still arguing and shoving, our guide led us around the edge of it and we slipped safely by to a hotel nearby.

At least two Arabs were killed and 120 persons injured in the shooting spree. The next day at least eleven Palestinians had been wounded by Israeli gunfire. Police stopped Arabs marching down the main streets of Jerusalem and arrested fifteen people.

By late afternoon on Sunday a measure of calm had returned to the Temple Mount. Employees took out all the carpets from the Dome of the Rock to clean them of shattered glass and to dry those that had been soaked when police flooded a cave under the Foundation Stone where they feared that the gunman may have had accomplices.

All Palestine had been ablaze. The incident at the mosque was the catalyst that touched off explosions of violence everywhere. In Jericho taxicabs were stoned; in Bethlehem gasoline bombs were thrown at cars; a crowd stoned a military patrol in Ramailah as news of the attack brought people out onto the streets in the West Bank. Youths stoned passing Israeli traffic and raised Palestinian flags. Troops fired on a mob in the West Bank town of Nablus. Troops in the Dalata refugee camp teargassed several hundred Arabs who had blocked the road with old refrigerators. Three youths were shot in the head at a demonstration at Dahaisha refugee camp in Bethlehem, where demonstrators had hurled rocks and set up flaming tire roadblocks.

Immediately after the incident in the square, the Muslim Supreme Council in Jerusalem called a general strike; it shut down the airports so that our tour group leaving from Jordan barely made it to Damascus, and later to Rome. It was the worst outbreak of violence since 1968, when the al-Aqsa Mosque was set aflame.

We were vastly relieved to get to a hotel for lunch and to ask the guide for an explanation for the disturbance. He was very noncommittal, and we learned practically nothing. He refused to talk any more, but warned us to go to our hotel and stay there. This advice was ignored—one group went to Bethlehem.

Following lunch we went to our hotel in West Jerusalem. I was accompanied on this tour by my sister, Merrie Claire Adler. She has been with me on many of my travels and has rendered invaluable assistance in times of emergency. Inasmuch as it was the time of the celebration of the Passover, the food in the Jewish hotels was different than usual. We had the usual kosher laws to observe, but other restrictions were imposed. We had taken it cheerfully, yet we were anxious for a variation in diet by this time in the tour.

In the afternoon of Easter Sunday, Mr. Emmanuel Dehan came up from Tel Aviv to visit with us. Mr. Dehan has been a friend of many years standing and we have toured with him, both privately and in group tours, over the length and breadth of Israel. Groups love him because he keeps them happy and enthusiastic during the whole trip. He is probably the most knowledgeable tourist guide in the State of Israel. He knows every inch of the land of Israel, having traveled the length and breadth since he was a child. At the present time he majors as a writer of guide books for Israel and has authored the beautiful travel book *Our Visit to Israel.*

Mr. Dehan is a master of English, French, German, and Hebrew, as well as six Arabic dialects. He was born in Galilee, a *Sabra,* the sobriquet for the native-born Israelis. *Sabra* means "cactus" — tough on the outside, tender on the inside. Mr. Dehan lost several of his family in the 1948 war, and at the present time is a reservist in the Israeli army. He always was armed on his travels. That day, fortunately, he was unarmed. Retaliation with a weapon on his part would have greatly escalated the incident I am going to describe. Emmanuel always maintained good relations with Arabs. I have seen him greet Arab friends many times with "bear hugs." He fraternizes as freely with them as he does with Israelis.

Sometimes it takes a tough *sabra* to be an Israeli guide. On one occasion Emmanuel was unloading baggage for his tour members at the border crossing between Israel and Jordan. While doing this he accidentally detonated a bomb that was in a suitcase. The explosion hurled him straight up in the air. He was bleeding profusely and was temporarily blinded. The staff at the crossing feared he was dead. They insisted that he be taken to the hospital, but, knowing that his absence would seriously disrupt the tour, he refused to go to the hospital. He wiped the blood off his clothes and face and continued to oversee the unloading of the baggage. Then he climbed on the bus to resume the tour, to the applause and wonder of the passengers.

That Easter Sunday was no different than any other Sunday to Emmanuel as he arrived from Tel Aviv. He was unaware of the fury that had been unleashed in the Square. He took us to the King David Hotel, the most prestigious in Jerusalem. The great King David has been eclipsed by the great hotels rising on the horizons of the new city. A modern Hyatt has been built at the foot of the Mount of Olives, and other elegant hotels are present, but the King David will always be the place where the VIPs go.

When we arrived, the hotel was experiencing a full house and a long waiting list. Emmanuel felt that we should go elsewhere — to the Intercontinental on the Mount of Olives, on the other side of the city, near East Jerusalem. The Intercontinental is now being listed as one of the historic hotels — patronized by the more affluent.

We engaged a taxi and set out for East Jerusalem. As we came near the Damascus Gate, Emmanuel noticed that there was a deadly, eerie quiet, unusual to this part of the city. It should have been wide open. Friday, not Sunday or Saturday, is the Muslim Holy Day. The stands, the peddlers, the crowds — all had vanished. The stores were all padlocked down as if expecting a hurricane. He immediately recognized the unusual nature of the area, but still did not sense the potential danger. We drove past the great Damascus Gate, so called because it opens out toward the north, toward Damascus. I also was aware of the abnormal atmosphere, but did not feel qualified to advise a man as experienced a guide as he was.

The Damascus Gate that long and fateful Sunday was empty of the usual tide of humanity. The traffic light was off, and little did we know that we were heading into a near fatal ambush. We went down around the Rockefeller Museum into the Valley of the Kidron, through some Arab repair shops, and headed up the Mount of Olives toward the Intercontinental Hotel.

We had crossed the Kidron Valley and were ascending the Mount of Olives. We were the lead taxi in a group which was going in the same direction. My sister was sitting in the front seat of the taxi,

Emmanuel Dehan was sitting near the door behind the driver, and I was sitting opposite him on the backseat. As we drew near to the Church of the Ascension, I noticed there were rocks scattered over the road. Immediately the thought crossed my mind that this resembled the streets of Belfast, North Ireland.

Suddenly a roaring torrent of rocks thundered on our taxi. The driver shielded his face with one hand and guided the taxi with the other. He never stopped moving. Had he stopped, the destruction could have been total. Behind us the other taxis were under the deadly rain of lethal rocks. All the pent-up hatred and frustration of the Arab mob, catastrophically induced by the attack at al-Aqsa Mosque, fell on us with devastating fury. My sister had dived down under the dash as the first impact crumbled the glass. The taxi continued to inch on under the fearful avalanche. Then it was over—momentarily. Suddenly the sky reverted to its normal brilliant blue—almost magically the mob melted away.

The only way that I can describe the next event is in photographic language. Having been a photographer for thirty years, it affords to me the most vivid portrayal of a sanguine episode, unsurpassed in my life. I had just raised myself up from my seat and had uttered my warning cry about the rocks scattered on the road. At that moment I saw a man standing by an olive tree, framed against the blue sky, as if I were looking through the viewing lens of a camera. At the very same instant I saw the frayed edges of a hole about the size of a baseball in the taxi window. The fact that they were so close together testifies to the incredible speed of the rock he had hurled at us. Then the lens closed, so to speak, and darkness descended upon me. The act of throwing and breaking seemed to be almost one. I collapsed unconscious between the seats. The rock had struck me on the left side of the face on my cheekbone and jaw. Blood was streaming from face and nose all over my clothing. (I was never able to clean the blood out of that beautiful shirt, which the missionaries had given me in the Philippines. I simply burned it.)

I later learned that a second mob of about fifty Arabs had rushed out from behind the Arab hospital, savagely beating with clubs and staves and iron bars on the taxi. The courageous Israeli taxi driver pressed right on through the storm until we arrived at the Intercontinental Hotel. The poor taxi driver's automobile was almost ruined. When we finally reached the Intercontinental I was lifted out and placed on the pavement. Beside me sat a young German tourist who had been hit in the head by a stone. Blood was streaming down her face in rivulets like crimson ribbons. It was a spectacular picture and was published nationally and internationally. Immediately my friends tried to get me into the Mount Scopus Hospital, which was the nearest. It was forty-five minutes before an ambulance could be secured, so great was the demand to care for the injured. I finally was brought to the Mount Scopus. As I lay there the reporters crowded around and the flashbulbs were blazing. My picture appeared the next day in one of the Jerusalem papers with that of the young girl, who was injured in the same attack. Finally, contact was made with the great Hadassah Hospital on the other side of the city. This is the largest hospital facility in the Middle East.

The van in which I rode was never meant to carry an injured person. It was very rough, and it seemed we would never arrive. Upon admission, I was taken immediately to the laboratory for X rays. This was a terrible ordeal. The man who was charged with pushing me in the cart took me down through a part of the hospital that was being remodeled. When he would come to a double door, instead of going before and gently opening it, he would bump it open with the cart. This caused excruciating pain in my head and face. I pleaded with him to stop this, but without success, as he didn't seem to understand any English. The procedure for taking X rays was nearly unendurable. There must have been at least thirty pictures taken of every angle. I was rolled from side to side, then over on my back, then on to my abdomen, then back again, over and over endlessly. When the ordeal was over, and I was wheeled up to meet the doctors who were on duty that night, they found that I had suffered several fractures of my lower jaw, and that my cheekbone and forehead were injured as well. They announced that they would have to wire the broken jaw shut. I was appalled at this decision, well aware of the pain and discomfort that would ensue. However, they said that it was too serious a decision for them to make — they would wait until morning to see the head doctor of the department. An angel was really with me at this juncture. Later on, when I had recuperated, I visited some of the people who had been injured in the same attack as I that Easter Sunday. They were Arab women, and they had their jaws wired shut. My condolences were only answered by a pitiful stare from the dark pools of their sad eyes.

The next day, Dr. J. Lewin Epstein, a graduate of the University of Pittsburgh and one of the top men in his field in the Middle East, arrived. To my immense relief, he announced after studying the X rays that he thought the jaw would heal without wiring, if I were careful and would refrain from moving it from side to side. This was, indeed, welcome news, but the cheekbones and forehead were much more seriously injured.

I had attempted, perhaps unwisely, to conceal the incident from my wife and family. I had hoped to get home without undue publicity, but my attempts failed. It was on the wires and on TV and soon the cameras were at our home interviewing my wife. She did a superb job under relentless questioning. Our area newspapers and the national press were carrying large headlines of the disaster on the Mount of Olives.

In the meantime I lay in the hospital, with all the facilities of a well-staffed, modern hospital at my disposal. The Hadassah occupies a commanding position on a hilltop not far from Ein Karem, the birthplace of John the Baptist. I had been there many times, but I had never dreamed that I would gaze at the lofty spire of its noble church from a hospital window.

The tourist company immediately went to work on my case. Israel has a special insurance fund covering acts of terrorism. There was a question whether there were enough funds to cover my case. I was under the constant supervision of a lady from the Tourist Institute who was working on my case to see that every need was met. I received condolences and flowers from the American Consul in Jerusalem, from the mayor of the city, from the Department of Tourism, and from many others. I was under the constant surveillance of a great team of doctors. Gradually I regained my strength. My sister remained the entire time with me. The hotel cancelled all charges and entertained her without charge during my hospital stay. After four days I was wheeled out beside the window of Marc Chagall into the brilliant sunlight.

A synagogue is a part of the hospital complex, and it is here that the famous Chagall windows can be seen. They are about eleven by eight feet each. Since Mosaic law forbids the representation of the human figure in art, Chagall had a restriction imposed on him, but he turned it to his advantage. He created a beautiful kingdom of stars and animals, the animals representing the twelve tribes of Israel. Basing his art on Genesis 49, where Jacob blesses the twelve tribes, Chagall used glass and color to magical effect. For many centuries artisans have created wonders in stained glass, but no one has ever succeeded so well as Chagall in this art. These windows were displayed for a short time at the New York World's Fair, and many visitors marveled at them. Now they are in Jerusalem, and I believe they can only be fully appreciated there.

When the time came to leave, all my expenses were borne by the Israeli government. They gave me countless courtesies and wonderful care, for which I shall be ever grateful. In fact, after I returned to America, a check for 2500 shekels, or about $210 in U.S. money, was mailed to me from the Insurance Institute. On the day of our departure, the Israeli Security picked us up with a car, collected our luggage, and took us to Tel Aviv. They handled our passports and tickets and put us on another airline so that we could rejoin our tour. This involved, they said, "bumping" two passengers to Copenhagen! I will be forever thankful for the insights I gained in this near tragic experience. Dr. Epstein said with some bitterness, "We treat 100,000 Arabs a year here, but they want to kill us."

Once more an angel had intervened. Had the rock struck one or two inches higher, this book would never have been written. In our national pastime of baseball, pitchers are often clocked at throwing a ball at 90 miles per hour. Some achieve perhaps 100 miles an hour. I am sure that the man who threw that deadly rock was approaching those speeds. A rock that could pierce plate glass and still have enough power to smash my face and render me unconscious must have been traveling at a tremendous rate of speed. But the angel softened the deadly blow!

While we experience such exhilarating comfort in the ministry of guardian angels, let us remember that they are messengers of the Godhead. They are awesome beings, fantastically powerful. As the end time approaches they will appear as the executors of God's judgments on an unrepentant, unbelieving universe. They are not God's hit squads, or a gang of terrorist beings let loose, but they are seen in majesty putting into action the divine decrees. A whole book could be written on the final acts of the angels in the Book of Revelation. They are God's administrators of the eternal plan:

"And I saw another mighty angel come down from heaven, clothed with a cloud: and a rainbow was upon his head, and his face was as it were the sun, and his feet as pillars of fire: And he had in his hand a little book open: and he set his right foot upon the sea, and his left foot on the earth, and cried with a loud voice, as when a lion roareth: and when he had cried, seven thunders uttered their voices. And when the seven thunders had uttered their voices, I was about to write: and I heard a voice from heaven saying unto me, Seal up those things which the seven thunders uttered, and write them not. And the angel which I saw stand upon the sea and upon the earth lifted up his hand to heaven, And sware . . . that there should be time no longer" (Rev. 10:1-6).

AFTERWORD

The imposing statue of Elijah upon Mount Carmel brandishing his victorious sword over the prostrate bodies of the priests of Baal dramatizes one of Scriptures most thrilling episodes in the eternal conflict of righteousness over sin. On this spot, they say, he demolished the pagan worship introduced into Israel by the wicked Phoenician queen, Jezebel. The huge rocks lying around remind you that it was twelve like these that Elijah gathered up in preparation for the great ordeal, and "he rebuilt the altar of the Lord that was broken down" (1 Kings 18:30). Elijah attempted to turn apostate Israel back to God and to achieve a national revival, but he found that he was struggling with a fickle and rebellious people. And Jezebel's bloody hand was clawing for him; she had sworn that the same fate was his that he had wreaked on her private college of false prophets.

I can see now the lonely, long-haired spectre below on the lovely plains of Jezreel, striped with fields of green and gold. He is fleeing for his life toward the south and the Negev. His strength has vaporized to weakness; his faith, once so dauntless, now is overwhelmed by the impending sword of Jezebel. One triumphant moment he had towered as a colossus among pygmies — one man against the world, and winning. The next he becomes a fugitive, forsaken and marked for destruction. Frustrated, weary, and dispirited, he says good-bye to his servant, goes a mile into the Negev and sits down under a *re'em*, or juniper tree.

The higher we go emotionally, the deeper, it seems, can be our fall. "Lord," he moans, "I've had enough. Take away my life, let me die." Elijah's destiny did not belong in the shallows, so he felt that life had tricked him, his goal had eluded him, the people who should have rallied to Jezebel's threat had forsaken him. The great victory, after all, had been lost. The triumph of Jehovah, after all, seemed only shallow and transient.

Then followed one of the most comforting passages in the Bible: "Behold, then, an angel touched him" (1 Kings 18:5). "Arise, O Elijah, God has still a work for you." Countless frustrated warriors in Christ's train have felt that divine angelic touch. Unearthly strength has flowed back into them, and they have arisen renewed and strengthened to scale the heights that once seemed insurmountable. The angels are still with us. The angel must have touched someone else, also, for under his guiding hand someone seeing the sleeping, exhausted prophet had placed a cake like the Bedouin eat, baked on coals of camel dung, and a cruse of water at his head. He would see it the very first moment when he awakened. That food would be enough for the desert traveler, for all the Bedouin has is that cake of dough and water to sustain him for weeks on end.

James tells us, "Take, brethren, the prophets for an example" (5:10). We certainly take them for an example of faith, but they are also instances of the agonizing frustration that often comes to the intense nature of the active enthusiast. *Prophets* are not *parrots* — they are a breed apart.

Take Daniel. After three weeks of fasting and prayer and discovering the prophecy hidden for ages from his nation, he lay exhausted upon his face asleep. An angel's hand touched him and set him upon his hands and knees trembling. He learned the amazing secret that answers to prayer can sometimes be delayed by unseen evil forces.

Ezekiel went at God's command "in the bitterness and heat of his spirit" and sat speechless for seven days among the captives by the rivers of Babylon. His mission was distasteful, and he knew it would be so ungratefully received and with deep hostility. But the hand of the angel was strong upon him. The angelic glory sustained him.

We take the example of the greatest of all prophets, Jesus Himself. Commentators have wrestled for ages with the mystery of Christ's prayer in Gethsemane. "Oh, my Father, if it be possible, let this cup pass from me" (Matt. 26:39). What was this cup? Had he become confused and frustrated? Was it fear of premature death before his work was finished? Had courage at last failed? Was it the horror of the trauma of Calvary?

We do know that at this tragic moment "there appeared an angel from heaven strengthening him" (Luke 22:43). How could an angel help the Son of God in His agony? Some have resolved this mystery by saying that it was only the human psyche of Jesus that struggled, while the fullness of the divine life withdrew itself. The great commentator Adam Clarke sums it up well when he says, "As to an angel strengthening Him, probably no more is meant by it than a friendly sympathizing of one of those heavenly beings with their Lord in distress; for what strength could the highest angel in heaven afford to our blessed Lord in His atoning acts? Surely none. The bare supposition is insupportable, but if we allow that the angel came to sympathize with Him during His passion, the whole account will appear plain and consistent."

We all know how precious the "friendly sympathizing" of a human being is in our hour of distress and frustration — just to hold our hand, to wipe away our tears, and stroke our brow. While "angels do not know the joy that our salvation brings," yet they are definitely "ministering spirits," even to the Lord of glory.

I had an evangelist friend who maintained that he was "God's pet." By that he meant that God had singled him out for some reason for special treatment. I certainly lay no claim to his, yet I cannot help but feel that in some situations in life I have been pleasantly surprised, and I could not help feeling that in them He had bade His holy angels watch after his frail child. Even in a day of technological marvels, we cannot help but feel needful. We cannot sustain ourselves. We were not meant to. We rely on the power of Almighty God, and we are pleased that His messengers and guardians are at work in the universe, guiding and protecting those who love the Lord.